the Tie that Binds

Nancy Otto Boffo & Linda Tomblin

the Tie that Binds

meditations for mothers and daughters

Cover photo by A. Santullo/The Stock Market

Scripture quotations marked KJV are from the King James or Authorized Version of the Bible.

Scripture quotations marked NRSV are from the New Revised Standard Version of the Bible, copyright © 1989. Used by permission.

Verses marked TLB are taken from THE LIVING BIBLE, © 1971 by Tyndale House Publishers, Wheaton, IL. Used by permission.

All Scripture quotations, unless otherwise indicated, are taken from the HOLY BIBLE, NEW INTERNATIONAL VERSION®. NIV®. Copyright © 1973, 1978, 1984 by International Bible Society. Used by permission of Zondervan Publishing House. All rights reserved.

Devotions marked N.O.B. are copyright © 1999 Nancy Otto Boffo
Devotions marked L.T. are copyright © 1999 Linda Tomblin

Published by Concordia Publishing House
3558 S. Jefferson Avenue, St. Louis, MO 63118-3968

Manufactured in the United States of America

Library of Congress Cataloging-in-Publication Data

Boffo, Nancy Otto, 1953-
    The tie that binds: meditations for mothers and daughters / Nancy Otto
Boffo and Linda Tomblin.
        p. cm.
    ISBN 0-570-05339-0
    1. Mothers—Prayer–books and devotions—English. 2. Daughters—
Prayer–books and devotions—English. 3. Christian women—Prayer–books
and devotions—English. I. Tomblin, Linda, 1941–   .
    II. Title.
    BV4847.B54   1999
    242'.643—dc21   99-11985
                                                              CIP

1 2 3 4 5 6 7 8 9 10   08 07 06 05 04 03 02 01 00 99

A cord of **three** *strands is not quickly broken.*

Ecclesiastes 4:12

To my mother, Patricia Otto, whose life, love, and faith has been my inspiration.

To my precious daughter, Jennifer. You are God's gift to me, and I love you with all of my heart.

To my husband, Mike, and our son, Matthew, for their unending support.

To my dear friends Pat Johnson and Flora Reigada for their valuable help and suggestions. And to Kathy Bisbee, Maureen Eaton, Martha Larchar, and Mike Mastroianni, who spent countless hours critiquing my manuscript.

I extend my heartfelt thanks to each of you. May God bless you always.

Nancy Otto Boffo

Together we dedicate our book to all mothers and daughters under the Son.

~ dedications

To my children—Robin, Mary, Katie, and Andy—who have given me the most wonderful gift of all—the opportunity to be their mother.

To Jenny and Frances, my "two" mothers—both necessary and both forever in my heart.

A special thank you to my husband, Earl, for his support of my writing projects.

Thank you, also, to our sons-in-law, Joe and Gary, who have helped make me the proud grandmother of grandsons Luke, Sam, Matthew, Ron, and Marcus and granddaughters Lydia, Jenny, and Heather. Each is a blessing from God.

And special appreciation to my daughter-in-law, Christy, who has lovingly become a fourth daughter, and to my two stepsons, Arthur and David, who have been sons to me from the very beginning.

Linda Tomblin

Contents

CHALLENGES

SPECIAL TIMES

A Letter to Our Readers

Dear Mothers and Daughters,

It is our heartfelt prayer that this devotional book will help strengthen the special God-given bond between mothers and daughters. We wanted to write this book not because we are best-selling authors, but because we have the "right" names—names with which you can relate—the simple names of both "Mother" and "Daughter." Having stood on both sides of the fence, we seek to share what we've learned with other mothers and daughters.

As you read about our joys and struggles, we believe that what God has revealed to us about our mother/daughter relationships—and our heavenly Father/daughter relationship—will help you in yours. While we understand that not all women have a good relationship with their mother or daughter, we hope that this book will bring you at least one step closer to a healthy and more meaningful relationship with each other.

To encourage communication and interaction between mothers and daughters of all ages, we've included "Love Knots" at the end of each chapter. These activities may spark a new interest or provide an opportunity to pull the two of you closer together.

Remember, a good relationship is a "team" effort. When mothers and daughters work together, play together, and share their faith with each other, God is in their midst. He is the third strand that strengthens the cord that binds mothers and daughters. And our desire is that these devotions will help transform the unique bond that you already share with your mother or daughter into "The Tie That Binds," thus bringing the two of you even closer together and closer to God.

In His love,
Nancy Otto Boffo and Linda Tomblin

DREAMS

Prayer

Lord of All Dreams,

You know how much I love my daughter, but I know that You love her even more. You knew her before she was conceived and loved her before she was born. You planned for her salvation from the beginning of time and kept Your promise to send a Savior.

Remind me that my dreams for my daughter might differ from hers or even clash with hers at times. Please give me the ability to see the difference between my expectations and her aspirations. Show me how to encourage the yearnings of her youth. Help me to be a mother who guides, supports, and inspires her daughter. Direct my actions and words as I point her to You as the source of her salvation and strength.

Let our dreams, both hers and mine, lift us higher than daydreams and make-believe and launch us closer to Your vision and goals for our lives. In Jesus' name. Amen.

What's So Special about a Girl?

God saw all that He had made, and it
was very good. Genesis 1:31

"Guess who's going to have a baby?" I asked Jennifer while she was coloring.

"You?" she questioned with wide open brown eyes.

"No, not me. Maureen," I answered.

"I guess she wants a girl since she already has two boys," Jennifer said. "Did you want a girl when I was born?"

Smiling, I sat down next to her at the table. "Yes, I did," I said. "I always wanted a daughter."

"Why? What's so special about a girl?" Jennifer asked.

As I stared into her questioning eyes, I wondered how I could explain the bond that ties a mother to her daughter. Thinking back to Jennifer's birth, I knew exactly how to answer.

"Jennifer, from the moment I first held you, I knew we'd share things that I'd never experience with Matthew."

Edging forward on her seat, Jennifer asked, "Like what?"

"Girl things—like brushing your hair and putting a pretty bow in it, polishing your nails, or trying on jewelry or dresses. I like to do those things," I answered.

"Yeah, I like to get dressed up," Jennifer said.

"You'll also experience the same feelings and body changes that happened to me. I'll be able to understand what you're going through and help you to understand it too," I added.

"We have a lot in common, don't we?" Jennifer asked.

"We sure do," I said as I put my hand on top of hers.

"And someday, you will be able to have a baby too."

Jennifer leaned over and hugged me. Smiling, she said, "Yeah, and I want to have a little girl!"

I smiled at her. All babies are gifts from God, but there's something special about a daughter. God has given me a unique connection with Jennifer that goes beyond mother-child. It is a love that grows with each joy and sorrow shared. Because we are both daughters of the same heavenly Father, we are connected through the saving love of Christ. And that is truly the tie that binds.

Heavenly Father, thank You for the things my daughter and I have in common—especially the faith You have given us and the promise of life eternal. May our relationship always be bound securely by the tie of Your love. In our Savior's name. Amen.

N.O.B.

God Knows What He's Doing

May He give you the desire of your heart
and make all your plans succeed.
Psalm 20:4

The first time Robin became pregnant, I was sure she'd have a girl. She always had wanted a daughter to dress in frilly clothes and show off. Instead, her first child was a healthy baby boy. Robin and Joe named him Luke. "God knew what He was doing," Robin told me. "A girl needs an older brother."

Luke was barely crawling when Robin found out she was pregnant again. Surely this time it would be a girl, we both thought. But it was another boy. Sam had snowy-white hair that did not change a bit as he grew older. "It's a shame a girl didn't get that hair," I often told him, but none of us would have traded the world for either boy.

"God knew what He was doing," Robin told me. "Because the boys are close in age, they will have similar interests and the same friends. It will work out well. And how wonderful that our little girl will have two older brothers."

Several years passed before Robin became pregnant again. By this time, Robin definitely was ready for some female companionship. She wanted someone that would have interests more like her own. She'd had about all the football, baseball, basketball, and car talk she could handle. She wanted someone who could appreciate fashion and fragrance, dresses and ribbons.

Around the third or fourth month, Robin had an ultrasound. When she saw the look on the doctor's face, she knew what he was going to say. "Robin, I know how much you want a girl—but this baby is definitely a boy," he said.

"Mama, I couldn't help it. I broke out in tears right there in the radiology department," Robin told me that afternoon. "I know it sounds like I'm being selfish—I am grateful to have a healthy child—but I've always dreamed of a ..." Her voice broke, and she changed the subject. From that point on, the family steered away from discussing the sex of the baby. Robin quietly exchanged the little pink dresses she'd already bought for pint-sized jeans and baby-boy blues.

We adjusted to the news and began considering names. "I think we'll name him Jimmy," Robin told me the week before she went into labor. The boys were excited about their new brother, and Joe already was planning to put a third seat in the go-cart. Before leaving for the hospital, Robin called to tell us they would be in touch once Jimmy arrived.

A few hours later, the phone rang. "Mama," Robin said, "it's over. I'm fine, and the baby's fine. But I do have one question."

"What is it?" I asked, relieved that my new grandson was safely here.

"How would you feel if we named the baby *Jenny* instead of *Jimmy*?" she asked.

"What do you mean?" I asked. Jenny had been my mother's name.

Robin couldn't contain her excitement any longer.

"The baby is a girl, Mama, a beautiful baby girl! The doctor can't explain it. The tests are usually accurate, but God had other plans."

Flabbergasted, I sank down on the chair next to the phone. "I think God proved to us one more time that He knows what He is doing!" I said. We both laughed for joy as we planned Jenny's homecoming.

> *Lord, remind me that even now You are looking out for my best interests, just as You did when You sent Jesus to be my Savior. Help me to put my total trust in You and to remember that my heart's desire is met by You alone. In Jesus' name. Amen.*

L.T.

I Want to Be Just Like ...

Her children arise and call her blessed.
Proverbs 31:28

The house was quiet except for the television program that Jennifer and I were watching. It was well past her bedtime, but that was okay. Because I had a part-time job, we didn't get too many opportunities to relax together. While she sat next to me, I stroked Jennifer's freshly shampooed hair, savoring this moment of togetherness.

On the program, two friends began arguing about who had the best mother. Jennifer shook her head and said, "Those girls are ridiculous."

"Why is that?" I asked.

"Because *I* have the best mommy," she said, smiling at me.

I hugged her close. "Thank you. I'm glad you think so," I said. She snuggled closer to me and continued to watch the show.

When the next commercial came on, Jennifer turned to face me. "You know, Mommy, I wouldn't mind if you turned out to be just like Grandma when you grow up," she said. "Grandma is so nice. When I have a bad dream at her house, she lets me come downstairs and we eat some pretzels. Then I feel better and don't have any more bad dreams."

"Is that why she's a good grandma?" I asked.

"There's more things than that. She makes me pretty

dresses, and she's never crabby. And I like the way she hugs me and tells me that she loves me." Jennifer looked up at me. "I think God made her real good."

Jennifer was right. God did make my mother "real good." Just like my daughter believes that I'm the best mommy in the world, I, too, think my mother is the greatest.

Of course, her attributes go beyond pretty dresses and pretzels. Mom's patience, faith, and integrity are all God-given traits that make her the Proverbs 31 woman that I admire. I treasure the trust and faith in the Lord that she demonstrates through word and action. I am thankful that she brought me up to know Jesus as my Savior. How well I remember her loving arms wrapped around me when I needed to be comforted after a bad dream or a bad day. And I remember the pretty dress I wore to my first dance and how Mom let me borrow her Nana's pin. And I'll never forget the smile on her face and the tears in her eyes when I handed her my newborn daughter—her first granddaughter.

What a blessing to be the daughter of such a godly woman. I pray that I can live up to Jennifer's expectations so I can be just like Grandma when I "grow up."

Thank You for my mother, Lord. Thank You for placing me in a Christian family with a mother who lives as Your child. Help me to demonstrate to my daughter the importance I place on living as Your daughter. May all that I do be pleasing in Your sight. In Jesus' name. Amen.

N.O.B.

When You've Reached a Goal, Then What?

"For I know the plans I have for you,"
declares the LORD, "… plans to give you
hope and a future." Jeremiah 29:11

Although Robin and Joe planned for their dream home from the day they were married, they knew the importance of small steps. First, they lived in a house trailer. Luke was born while they lived there. Then they bought a small house, a smart choice because their second son, Sam, was born not long afterward. Joe added a deck to the house, and Robin made drapes for the windows and stenciled borders in each room. They planted flowers and turned the red dirt yard into a carpet of green. Then Jenny was born, a dog and a cat were added, and their home was bulging with life.

Robin and Joe decided to move forward with plans for their dream home. They bought a plot of land and made plans with a contractor. When they put their home on the market, the house sold immediately. They had to move into a two-bedroom apartment with the three children, the dog, and the cat while construction of the new home was completed.

Robin and Joe made friends with the neighbors at the apartment complex, shared their room with Jenny and the cat, put the boys and the dog in the other bedroom, and looked forward to the future. After work each day, Joe went to the homesite and helped the carpenters. Robin pored over decorating books, made more drapes and slipcovers, and dreamed of having space to herself once again.

Finally the day came. Robin and Joe moved into their brand-new two-story, four-bedroom, brick house. Everything was put in the place that had been planned for it. The children removed their shoes at the door to keep the new carpet clean and stored their toys in rooms of their very own.

Everything was picture perfect, but for some reason, no one seemed quite satisfied. Joe kept looking for something to do. The boys lay on their individual beds and watched their individual television sets. And Jenny refused to sleep in her room, which had been lovingly decorated with bright colors and carousel horses.

"I just can't figure it out," Robin told me when I stopped by for a visit. "Something just doesn't feel right."

"But the house is the way you planned it, isn't it?" I said, looking around. "The children have large rooms. There's a basement where Joe can work on his projects. And you even have a beautiful garden tub in your bathroom with a stained-glass window over it just like you've always wanted. What more could you ask for?"

"I don't know," she said. "We seemed happier in the other house and the apartment. Even the trailer seemed more 'right' somehow."

"Remember when you were graduating from high school?" I asked. "You had dreamed of going to high school since you were a little girl, then it was suddenly over. You felt sad that part of your life was ending. When you got into college and had new plans and dreams, life took on a new glow."

I picked up a framed poem that was sitting on the bookshelf beside the fireplace. "Do you remember this?" I asked.

"Sure," Robin said and smiled. "It's the poem you wrote for my graduation."

"Could it be that your family needs to find new dreams?" I asked as I read. *"Captured stars sometimes dim in the light of the sun./Stretch up once more beyond the light./Still a bit beyond reach are other stars just as bright.*

"God has blessed you with a wonderful family. He guided you and Joe as you planned for this house and worked to make it happen," I said. "Now He will help you choose new paths and make new plans."

"You're right. God has been good to us," Robin said. "And we do need something new to look forward to—another star."

It wasn't long until everyone in the family had a new "dream." Robin was taking a class in watercolors at the local college. Joe was looking forward to a trip to California for a work-related seminar. The boys had begun construction on a clubhouse with their new friends from the neighborhood. And Jenny ... Well, Jenny still wouldn't sleep in her room, but she had started school and had an abundance of dreams tucked away in her head.

Lord, remind me that You are the molder of my dreams. You give them to me when they are conceived, and You bring them to fulfillment. Thank You for both! And when my earthly future seems cloudy or the direction of my life seems unclear, remind me that You have prepared a glorious future for me in heaven with You. In Jesus' name. Amen.

L.T.

Who Am I?

You created my inmost being; You knit
me together in my mother's womb. ...
Your works are wonderful.
Psalm 139:13–14

Because most of our relatives live a great distance from us, Jennifer hasn't spent as much time with them as children whose aunts and uncles live nearby. Therefore she doesn't always grasp family relationships.

When Jennifer was very young and received Christmas or birthday gifts in the mail, she would ask, "Who is this from?" but she didn't always make the connection. She would repeatedly ask: "Who is Aunt Ellen?" or "Is Aunt Cathy married to Uncle Marty or to Uncle Joe?" I had to remind my little girl that her Aunt Ellen is my sister and that Aunt Amy is married to Uncle Joe and that Aunt Cathy is married to Uncle Marty.

One rainy afternoon, in an effort to help Jennifer understand her bond to these unfamiliar family members, I pulled out some photographs. I thought this might help her to see who went with whom and eventually come to recognize names and faces. We cuddled on the couch as we went through the albums. I told my daughter who each person was and how she was related to him or her.

When we finished, I picked out a picture of my parents and my grandparents to show Jennifer my family line.

"Wow, you look a lot like Grandma," Jennifer marveled

as she glanced back and forth from the photograph to me. "Who do I look like?"

"I think you have some features from both Daddy's side of the family and from mine. Here, look at this picture." I flipped to one of her baby pictures and to a picture of my mother-in-law. I pointed out the strong resemblance.

Jennifer sat quietly for a moment. "If I look like everyone else, who am I?" she asked.

I took my precious little girl in my arms and gave her a hug. "You're you—Jennifer Marie Boffo. And though you may look a little like some of your relatives, God made you different and special."

"Do you mean I'm still me, even though there are parts of everyone else inside of me?" Jennifer asked.

"Sure. It's like when we make chocolate-chip cookies," I said, smiling. "We take a lot of good things like chocolate chips, walnuts, sugar, and eggs and mix them all together. When we get done, we have a delicious cookie.

"It's the same with you," I said. "God took some of His most favorite things from our family and mixed them all into you. And that's what makes you my special little cookie!"

Jennifer giggled and gave me a kiss. "Thanks, Mommy," she said. "You know what? I'm hungry—and *all* of me wants to eat!"

O Creator God, I'm so thankful that I know who I am, and I know Whose I am. Thank You for making me Your precious daughter, forgiving all my sins through the saving work of Your Son. Help me to use my unique gifts to serve You. In Jesus' name. Amen.

N.O.B.

Love without Boundaries

Therefore, as God's chosen people, holy and dearly loved, clothe yourselves with compassion, kindness, humility, gentleness and patience. Bear with each other and forgive whatever grievances you may have against one another. Forgive as the Lord forgave you. And over all these virtues put on love, which binds them all together in perfect unity.
Colossians 3:12–14

Katie has loved animals from the day she was born. I can't even count the number of dogs, cats, rabbits, ducks, baby chicks, parakeets, canaries, and cockateels that have graced our lives because of her. But out of all these animals, her biggest dream was to own a toy poodle.

One night I came home from work with a snow white bundle of fur tucked inside my coat. Katie named the poodle *Teddy* because he looked like a teddy bear.

Teddy never left Katie's side. He protected Katie from imaginary beasts when she was in first grade, lay by her side as she studied algebra in junior high, listened patiently to her boyfriend problems in high school, and loved her when she felt no one else in the world understood her.

Teddy still sleeps on Katie's bed and knows the sound of her car when it turns onto the road to our house, he is her baby, her confidant, and the one earthly friend she knows will never desert her. He is getting old now—he has lost most of his teeth, has gone deaf, and is practically blind—but Teddy acts like a young pup when Katie is around.

One morning, I let Teddy outside only to find that he had not returned within the customary 15 minutes. I called for him to no avail. When Katie came down for school, she called him, but Teddy was nowhere in sight.

Then the phone rang. Our neighbor said he had seen Teddy on the highway—he'd been hit by a car. When my husband brought Teddy back to our house, the dog was not fully conscious. We decided our pet probably had internal injuries and would have to be put to sleep. But, surprisingly, the veterinarian said he only had a concussion.

For the next two weeks, Teddy remained in the animal hospital hooked up to an IV. While he was at the hospital, Katie spent every minute she could with Teddy. She loved him despite his attempt to run away and the scare he had given her. When he returned home, she helped him up on the bed when he was woozy and coached him to eat.

I think that the love Katie expresses for Teddy and he for her must be a little like the unlimited love God shows to us. We sinned and roamed far from God. We thought we could make it on our own. But God loved us even though we were sinners. Out of His boundless mercy, He sent His only Son to win us back. Jesus gave His life on the cross to redeem us, to bring us into God's family forever. His resurrection assures us of a place in God's heavenly kingdom.

What a gift to share God's love with my daughter—to know that I can forgive her because my heavenly Father has forgiven me, to know that we are bound together in Him.

Holy Father, thank You for Your abundant, inexhaustible, boundless love as demonstrated in Jesus. Strengthen my love for my daughter and keep us both close to You. In Jesus' name. Amen.

L.T.

A Dream Come True

Be still, and know that I am God.
Psalm 46:10

I was devastated—again. This month was no different
from the one before and the one before that. I wasn't pregnant.

I had tried hard not to think that this would be the
month for our dream to come true. I had tried to go about
the business of living, enjoying my wonderful husband and
our healthy son, Matthew. But it was hard, almost impossible, to do. Although I knew that God's timing was perfect, I
was growing tired of being patient. In fact, after many years
of thermometers, charts, tests, surgery, and pills, my patience
was just about gone.

It wasn't fair! I'd already conceived one child. Why was
it so difficult to have another? I dreamt about having a
daughter to complete our family. I wanted a little girl, a
daughter with whom I could shop, whisper secrets, and
enjoy womanhood. And I wanted her now!

I threw my basal temperature chart against the wall.
Tears streamed down my face as I collapsed on my bed.
"Why, God, why?" I cried. I pounded the bed with my fists
and cried until I could cry no more. That was it. I'd had it!
No more charts, no more pills, no more …

I give up, God. I can't take this roller coaster ride anymore.
Whatever You want—I don't care anymore, I thought.

Relinquishing my dream felt good but only for a while.

Soon my desire to have a daughter returned. I talked to my husband about adoption, but he wasn't willing to adopt. It seemed that my dream would never come true. But deep down inside, I knew God had a plan for our family, so I continued to hope and to pray.

A few months later, Mike confided that he had a "little talk" with God. He had asked God to help him to love another person's child as his own. Mike agreed that we could look into adoption. But before we did, a miracle happened—I became pregnant! God had answered my prayers. He hadn't given up on me—even if I had given up on my dream.

The next few months passed in a blur. Since Matthew was born prematurely, my pregnancy was considered high risk. I had numerous doctor's appointments and tests. Our joy turned to horror when I began spotting. With bed rest and surgery, the immediate danger passed. Now confined to my bed for the remainder of my pregnancy, I prayed unceasingly for God to spare the life of my child.

More complications followed, however, and I was admitted to a hospital with a neonatal intensive care unit. But joy of joys, an ultrasound clearly showed that I was carrying a baby girl! Since Mike and I already had picked out her name, I began talking to my bulging stomach and calling Jennifer Marie by name.

I spent eight weeks in a hospital bed, awaiting my daughter's arrival. On August 22, 1985, Jennifer was born, weighing in at four pounds, 15 ounces. Although she was almost five weeks premature, my baby girl was healthy!

When I finally got to hold her in my arms, I counted Jennifer's fingers and toes. Each was perfectly made, and I admired the intricacy of God's handiwork. My heavenly Father, the One who gave me physical life and the promise of eternal life through His Son's work on the cross, had once again bestowed the gift of motherhood on me. And He had granted me my heart's desire—He had given me a daughter.

As I watched her sleep, I dreamt of all the fun times to come. Once again, tears streamed down my face. But this time, they were tears of joy and thanksgiving.

O God of mercy and love, thank You, thank You for entrusting me with a daughter. Help me to be a good mother as I raise my daughter to know and love You. In Jesus' name. Amen.

N.O.B.

A Dream Diet

Therefore I tell you, do not worry about
your life, what you will eat or drink....
Is not life more important than food?
Matthew 6:25

Though I don't like to admit it, I have at one time or
another been on every kind of diet—the carbohydrate diet,
the protein diet, the banana diet, the soup diet, the juice
diet, the 12-snacks-a-day diet—not to mention a member of
every weight-loss organization in town.

It seems like every time my daughters and I go somewhere, I'm on some kind of diet. And whatever they want
to eat is the exact opposite of what I can eat. When we
went to New York, it was protein time. While they feasted
on hot pretzels and mustard, yummy rolls with butter melting down the sides, and incredible vegetable and fruit con-
coctions, I ate boiled eggs and hard cheese. Several weeks
later we went on our yearly Christmas shopping spree. My
daughters ate a marvelous breakfast of omelets with creamy
cheese and bacon while I ate unsweetened breakfast rolls.
(It was carbohydrate week, after all.)

But I finally have listened to my daughters' diet philoso-
phy. They eat a balanced diet, eat only when hungry, and
stop eating when they are full. This may make much more
sense than putting my body and mind through turmoil.
Once again I can enjoy food without feeling guilty.

As I reflect on my diet efforts, it amazes me how much

energy I spend on things that have no eternal value. If I spent only a quarter of the time with my Lord that I spend counting calories, how much the better! My heavenly Father desires that I dine daily on His Word and spend time frequently at His Table where I receive the life-giving body and blood of His Son, who was sacrificed for me that I might have life eternally.

God also wants me to enjoy fruitful earthly relationships. That's why my girls and I have put together a dream diet for mothers and daughters.

1. Eat lunch together once a week.

2. Gather at mom's for Sunday dinner.

3. Occasionally throw in an "anything goes" omelet and pancake breakfast.

4. And do it all in moderation (except the giggling)!

Father, thank You for the fun times, the times I spend with my daughters as friends. Make me willing to learn from them—and to pass on to them the things I have learned about You. Send Your Spirit to work in me a hunger for Your life-giving Word and Sacrament. In Jesus' name. Amen.

L.T.

Who Is Prince Charming Anyway?

Husbands, love your wives, just as
Christ loved the church and gave Himself
up for her. Ephesians 5:25

When Jennifer was 4 years old, she loved to wear dress-up clothes and pretend she was a princess or a bride. She spent hours talking to her dolls while acting out different scenarios.

One day I heard the rustle of plastic in my closet, then a pint-sized voice crying, "Ooohhh, aaahhh ... Mommy, come here!"

I knew right away what that meant. Jennifer had found my wedding dress.

"Can I see it?" she begged.

I took the dress out of the plastic bag. Jennifer reverently touched the lace and the beads. "It's so pretty. Can I wear it when I get married?"

"Sure, if it fits you," I said. "So who are you going to marry?"

"I don't know. But I want him to be handsome and nice."

"And what else?" I asked.

"He needs to have a job so we can get food and a puppy," Jennifer answered.

"A puppy?" I asked. Jennifer just giggled. We talked for a while about the qualities we thought her Prince Charming should possess. Later, I took out my wedding album and we enjoyed looking at the photographs.

Over the years, Jennifer and I have had many conversations about the man she may someday marry. As she has matured, so has the content of our discussions. At first, I would ask if "nice" meant that Prince Charming would be kind to animals as well as to her. Later, it came to mean that he would cater to her every wish and lavish her with gifts as well as his devotion.

Although these qualities once sounded perfect to my daughter, she has grown to realize that these qualities are less than realistic. As Jennifer has experienced life, friendships, and relationships with boyfriends, she has realized that the most important thing she can look for in a guy is his relationship with the Lord.

My dreams for Jennifer include a husband straight out of the fifth chapter of Ephesians. I want her to marry a man who puts God first in his life and who loves his wife as Christ loves the church.

I want my only daughter to spend the rest of her life with a man who believes that his marriage vows are a sacred bond that is not to be broken. I want to know that infidelity and divorce are not an option for the man to whom my daughter has given her heart and her life.

I want them to go to church together, pray together, study God's Word together, and be there for each other through thick and thin. And when children arrive, I want Mr. Right to be a daddy who helps, nurtures, and enjoys the precious gifts born from their love. I want him to be a Christian man and father that I will be proud to call my son.

Besides looking for these godly qualities in a man, I've tried to make Jennifer aware of something else. Since no man is perfect and everyone falls short of our expectations, I want my daughter to remember that the only One who can meet all her needs is Jesus. He will never fail or forsake her. Since He always will be by her side, I want Jennifer to lean on the Living Christ who has already won for her the forgiveness of sins and the promise of eternal life. Because of Christ, Jennifer can forgive even as she has been forgiven by God.

It will be exciting to help Jennifer plan her wedding to the man of her dreams. Whether she wears my wedding dress doesn't matter as much as whom she marries. May God guide her to choose wisely.

O Jesus, I know You want the best for my daughter. Please guide her in all her relationships. In Your perfect timing, lead her to a godly man whose love for her will mirror Your love for us. Amen.

N.O.B.

One Thing I Seek

*I press on toward the goal to win the
prize for which God has called me heav-
enward in Christ Jesus. Philippians 3:14*

I remember a paper Katie wrote for a high school
English class. The teacher probably doesn't remember it.
Katie probably doesn't remember it. But I'm sure Mary
always will remember it.

The students were asked to write about the person they
most admired. Katie thought for a long time before she
decided on the subject for her paper. Naturally, I came up
with several suggestions: a teacher who had been particularly helpful, a pastor who had been there for our family, or the
physical therapist at the clinic where Katie had worked the
previous summer.

Katie didn't seem to like any of these suggestions.
When she began work on the paper, she didn't ask for any
assistance, so I left her alone. But I couldn't help wondering
whom she had chosen. Maybe it was her best friend or one
of the doctors whose children she'd been baby-sitting for
several years.

I was surprised Katie didn't ask me to read the paper
when she had finished. Instead, she put it inside a folder
and stuck it in her book bag. I forgot about it, and life took
on the familiar routine of homework and housework.

A month or so later, Katie came across the paper as she
was cleaning out her book bag. "Oh, you might want to read

this," she said. "The teacher said it was good." She passed it over to me as she continued dragging chewing gum wrappers and eraser-less pencils from her bag.

"The person I most admire," the paper began, "is my sister Mary." Katie described how Mary had married young, given birth to a beautiful baby boy, and left high school classmates behind in favor of a family and adult responsibilities. "But she went to the local community college and completed courses to earn her high school diploma," Katie wrote. "She finished high school while taking care of a home and child, and then went on to take college courses." In her conclusion, Katie wrote, "I know it hasn't been easy. Mary's missed many good times—the proms and ball games and graduation with her class—but she's gained many advantages in the long run—a spirit of determination and a strong work ethic, not to mention the admiration of her younger sister."

I convinced Katie to let Mary read the paper. "Of course, you know it was just because I was in a hurry and needed someone to write about," Katie told Mary with a laugh after Mary finished reading the paper.

"That's what I figured," Mary said, giving her sister a playful push. But for a split second before the jokes began, I noticed tears in Mary's eyes and love and pride on Katie's face.

I'm sure Mary regretted that she couldn't finish school with her classmates. I know at times that it seemed like she always was trying to catch up with the rest of the world. Katie's paper confirmed to Mary that she is a fine Christian young woman who has earned her way in the world—and the respect of her family and friends. Success is sometimes spelled differently for different people.

Paul says that we "[strain] toward what is ahead" (Philippians 3:13). We do this in our daily lives as we set goals and do our best to achieve them despite difficult circumstances. We do this in our spiritual lives when we ask the Holy Spirit to strengthen our faith and point us to those things God would have us do. The Holy Spirit working in us motivates us to "press on" so our words and actions become more Christ-like, even as our Lord "pressed on" to the cross to rescue us from our sins and win for us eternal life.

I am proud of each of my daughters. Though they are all different, they are alike in their love for God, their families, and each other. These Christian women have their eyes firmly on the prize God has called them to—life eternal with Him.

Father, I pray the words of Psalm 27 for myself and for my daughters: "One thing I ask ... this is what I seek: that I may dwell in the house of the LORD all the days of my life, to gaze upon the beauty of the LORD and to seek Him in His temple." Thank You that I can trust You to "keep me safe in [Your] dwelling; ... hide me in the shelter of [Your] tabernacle and set me high upon a rock." In Jesus' name. Amen.

L.T.

Hat Tricks

I am confident ... that the one who began
a good work among you will bring it to
completion by the day of Jesus Christ.
Philippians 1:6 (NRSV)

When Jennifer was about 3 years old, her brother gave her his well-worn box of costume hats for pretend play. Matthew had received it years earlier as a gift from his aunt and uncle. He'd enjoyed pretending that he was a firefighter, astronaut, cowboy, police officer, and a great hunter on safari. Now that he was 9 years old, he no longer played make-believe. Since his little sister had often sneaked into his room to "borrow" a hat, he knew she would enjoy his gift.

One day Jennifer walked into the kitchen wearing the cowboy hat. She had tied a red bandanna around her neck and put on the sheepskin vest her grandmother had sewn for Matthew when he was in preschool.

"Guess what I am," my daughter stated proudly.

I furrowed my brow and remained quiet for a moment. "Are you a cowgirl?" I finally asked.

"Yup," she said, pleased that her role was recognizable. "Do you wanna see my horse?"

I nodded yes. Jennifer led me to her bedroom where she got on her rocking horse and "rode the range"—just to impress me, I'm sure. "You certainly are a great cowgirl," I said when she finished rocking back and forth.

"Yes, I know. And do you know what? I'm gonna be a cowgirl when I grow up, and I'm gonna have lots of horses and sheep." She smiled and nodded for emphasis and went back to galloping across the wild west of her dreams.

As I rode away from the OK Corral and returned to the reality of washing the breakfast dishes, I thought about how much I loved horses when I was growing up and how I dreamed of having my own horse. I felt blessed that my dream had come true. I prayed that Jennifer could experience the joy of owning one of God's most magnificent animals, if that would still be her dream as an adult.

But everything changed the following week when Jennifer donned the space explorer hat. Since we live on the Space Coast of Florida, rocket and shuttle launches are commonplace to my little 21st-century would-be explorer. Day after day she flew off to faraway places and discovered new worlds that even Captain Kirk and Mr. Spock had never seen. Now she was determined to become an astronaut, and she promised that she would wave to me as her spaceship passed over our house!

Needless to say, Jennifer's dream career has changed many times. That old box of hats gave her the opportunity to make-believe that she truly was involved in many occupations. Now that Jennifer is in seventh grade, she has moved beyond play hats and has begun to consider seriously what "real" hats she may want to wear.

My son's search for a college and a career path has prompted my daughter and me to discuss the many choices available to her. I've pointed out to Jennifer her strengths and weaknesses. Helping her to recognize what subjects she enjoys or what God-given talents she possesses may help her to decide what her dream job will be.

Perhaps she'll discover that she will wear many hats, as I do. I fill the roles of cook, housekeeper, nurse, teacher, accountant, secretary, chauffeur, and counselor, among others. I am also an author, speaker, free-lance writer, and bookkeeper. Some of these roles are ones that I never dreamed I would pursue. Others I've had to work long and hard to achieve, constantly asking God for His guidance and support.

But the most important thing is that my daughter knows that God has a plan and a purpose for her life. The Bible tells us that before we were formed in our mother's womb, God knew us (Jeremiah 1:5). The Lord says to each of us, "I know the plans I have for you … plans to prosper you and not to harm you, plans to give you hope and a future" (Jeremiah 29:11).

The God who formed the universe created my daughter and me and planned for our salvation through the life, death, and resurrection of His only Son. Through the gift of faith, we are daughters of the King, with a future place in heaven. He who began a good work in us will see it to completion. Through His Holy Spirit, God strengthens our trust in Him and enables us to follow His course. As we follow His leading, we find that the "hat" He has chosen for us fits exactly.

Almighty God, You are the "author and perfecter of [my] faith" (Hebrews 12:2). Help me to trust Your plan for my life and the life of my daughter. In Jesus' name. Amen.

N.O.B.

The Trip of a Lifetime

Great is our LORD and mighty in power;
His understanding has no limit.
Psalm 147:5

Each of my daughters is like me in some way, but Katie is probably the only one who longed to travel abroad as much as I did. I was thrilled when her high school Spanish teacher decided to take the class on a three-week trip to France and Spain. While it sounded like the trip of a lifetime, it turned into an unexpected source of worry for me.

First, we had to finance the trip. After that was settled, clothes needed to be bought. Then came the "But, Mom, I need …" and the "I have to have …" and the "We're required to have …" purchases; trip cancellation insurance, baggage insurance, extra medical insurance; more money for side trips; and money for food and souvenirs.

When all the monetary issues were solved, I thought my worries were over. Actually they were far from over. Have you ever put your daughter on an airplane to travel halfway around the world with other teenagers and a teacher who looks and acts just as young?

Katie called every few days and seemed to be having a wonderful time. I managed to survive those three weeks … until I realized her teacher was staying in France while the kids returned home alone. Somehow I had missed this tidbit of information. I was on pins and needles. They would have to maneuver around Europe, land in Washington D.C., and transport themselves to another airport to catch another plane to Charlotte.

I could hardly wait to make the two-hour drive to the airport to pick up Katie and her friend. Before we left, however, the parents of Katie's friend called to volunteer to pick up the girls. After all, they were going to Charlotte anyway. I assumed they had spoken with the girls and made all the arrangements. Although I was disappointed, I decided it would save us a long trip, and Katie probably would feel more grown-up and independent if we weren't waiting anxiously when she got off the plane.

When Katie arrived home later that night, she was exhausted but thrilled by the trip. She gave us the souvenirs she'd bought and fell into bed (where she stayed for the next 14 hours).

It wasn't until sometime later that I learned Katie had been disappointed that we weren't there to meet her plane. Her friend had made the arrangements for the ride home, and Katie assumed that we hadn't wanted to make the drive. It also turned out that she had missed us as much as we had missed her, but she couldn't say so with her friends nearby.

We soon cleared up the misunderstanding, but it showed us how easily feelings can be hurt, even when neither party intends for this to happen.

It's a good thing God understands us better than we understand each other. He knows even our inner sins, yet in His perfect love, He sent Jesus to lead us back to Him. He will help us to love one another and to forgive one another, even as He loves and forgives us for Jesus' sake.

Lord, let us never forget that our relationships with each other are gifts from You. May we treat them with care and never take anything for granted. Amen.

L.T.

Caution: Wet Cement

For a man's ways are in full view of the
LORD, and He examines all his paths.
Proverbs 5:21

"Let's go for a walk, Mommy," Jennifer begged. We had
been confined to our house for two days because of torren-
tial rains. I had to agree that the blue skies and morning sun
seemed to beckon us.

"Okay, let's go," I told my 4-year-old.

The smell of clean, crisp air greeted us when we stepped
outside. Since it was early, our neighborhood was quiet.
With nothing to distract us, we sauntered down the sidewalk, appreciating the world around us.

During our walk, I pointed out a squirrel that was running across the telephone wires and a bird that was taking a
bath in a puddle. Jennifer quietly took in all the sights and
sounds.

A little while later, my daughter stopped to look at the
sidewalk. "Look," she said, "it's a leaf."

Since I didn't see any leaves around us, I asked her to
point out her discovery. My preschooler pointed to the sidewalk, then got down on her knees. I crouched beside her, my
eyes searching the area for a leaf. Finally, I saw what she was
talking about. Preserved in the cement was the form of a leaf.

Jennifer traced the indentation with her finger and
looked up at me. "How did it get there?" she asked.

I explained how a leaf had been caught in the wet

cement and had left its mark. As we looked at another spot
in the sidewalk, we saw some animal footprints and someone's
initials scrawled on the outer edge. Wherever we looked, visi-
ble signs of animals and humans had been left behind.

Life is like that sidewalk. As we walk along in life, we
leave our mark on people and on their hearts. What we say
or do can leave an impression that will stay with someone
for the rest of his or her life.

As a mother, I have an awesome responsibility. My children are like wet cement and it's my privilege to ensure that
my actions make a positive impact on their impressionable
lives. I need to be careful of what I say and do so I will benefit and nurture, not tear down and weaken.

How do I do this? How do I become the "good" mother
that I've dreamed of being? I turn to the Bible for guidance
and to God through prayer. Jesus left us an example that is
perfect, and His life and message still impact our lives today.
He tells us in John 13:15, "I have set you an example that
you should do as I have done for you."

Although we will never be perfect, we can ask the Holy
Spirit to help us follow God's commands and imitate
Christ's life. We can be assured that God will help us leave
impressions on the "sidewalks" of our family and friends that
will be pleasing. And when we make the wrong choices,
God is there with the assurance of His love and forgiveness
for Jesus' sake.

*Dear Lord, I pray that Your light shines through me so
the mark I leave behind glorifies Your holy name. In
Jesus' name. Amen.*

N.O.B.

We All Need a Role Model

Follow my example, as I follow the
example of Christ. 1 Corinthians 11:1

My Aunt Frances was always like another mother to
me. Actually, she was more like my mother at times. She
and Uncle Marshall invited me to live with them when I
finished high school. They introduced me to people at their
church. They helped me find my first job.

I had never lived in a house or a family like theirs.
Their home was beautiful, decorated with fine furniture and
furnishings I'd only dreamed about. And everyone got
along. They actually acted as if they liked one another.
Although I loved my mother and got along well with her
and my brother, my stepfather was another matter. There
was no getting along with him. I tried to stay out of his way.

Frances and Marshall both worked to turn their small
gas station and automobile repair business into one of the
best in Gastonia. Their fondness for people was apparent to
everyone—customers included. Before long, businesses were
sending their fleets to the station for service.

When I was young, Frances had beautiful, dark, curly
hair; a trim figure; and a grace that made me dream of being
like her when I grew up. Marshall always was laughing and
joking, making sure that the children had fun. They took
Dan and me on vacations with their family and invited us
to stay with them for the summers.

When Marshall developed Alzheimer's, Frances kept

him at home as long as she could. When she had to place him in a nursing center, Frances spent most of each day caring for him. Before long, Frances was asked to head the Families Group for the hall in which Marshall's room was located. She spent even more time at the center, voluntarily assisting the other families or the patients who had no one. Frances was at the home every day for more than two years until Marshall died.

A year or so ago, I received a call from Frances' sons, Tim and David. "Mom's been in an accident," they said. "It's serious." I called Robin, and we went immediately to the hospital to see Frances. We visited her in the intensive care unit. Although she spoke to us, it was obvious Frances didn't know who we were.

"How is she?" I asked my cousins when we went back to the waiting room.

"Not good," David replied. "She's already had major surgery—when they brought her in, she had internal injuries. Now they've got to make more repairs. She's so weak … they say she may not make it through the surgery."

"And if she does," Tim said, swallowing hard, "it's going to be a long hard, recovery. She'll have to have someone with her all the time."

Knowing that they both lived a great distance away, I told them I'd stay with her whenever necessary.

"I've got to tell you what she did when the ambulance brought her here," Tim said. "She was all alone, in terrible pain, and they were trying to get her to sign to go into surgery. She refused to let them put her under until they got in touch with her preacher. When he arrived and prayed with her, she finally gave them permission to operate."

"Sounds like a pretty 'strong' person to me," I said. I smiled to think of the witness she had given.

God was with Frances and the medical team. She came through the second surgery and entered a recovery phase that lasted almost six months. God was with her throughout the recovery just as He had been with her in the hospital. This unexpected medical situation gave all of us who loved Aunt Frances the opportunity to give back to a woman who always had given so much of herself. When David and Tim couldn't be with their mother, I stayed with her. And if I had to leave, two women who lived next door volunteered their time. And when everyone else had to work, Aunt Frances' cousin would visit until someone could return.

It was a frightening time for all of us, but I had the opportunity to give back to my Aunt Frances for all that she had done for me. And through the process, I believe I began to fulfill my dream to "be like her when I grow up." I didn't suddenly grow dark, curly hair or change my short, slightly overweight body for her tall, slender frame, but I know God was at work in me to make my heart and spirit more like hers—more in line with that of a servant.

Father, help me to realize the importance of family and friends—and the important role I play in their lives. Teach me to be more like You and more like those special people in my life who give unselfishly of themselves. Through Your Holy Spirit, remind me again that Your Son gave Himself selflessly for me and all sinners that we might live as Your children in service to others. In my Savior's name. Amen.

L.T.

Dare to Dream

1. **Dream about the future.** Talk to the special women in your life once a year about your dreams—the "I wishes" or "I want tos." Define her interests and dreams and share your own dreams, both past and present. Tape the discussion or write down the main ideas. Review last year's dreams. Discuss how you saw God at work in each other's lives to fulfill dreams or encourage new ones. Ask God to continue to bless your plans and guide you to do His will. Plan how to encourage and accomplish dreams. Place several on your calendar.

2. **Dream about planting a seed.** Plant a garden with your daughter. Allow her to pick out the flowers, vegetable seeds, or plants she's always wanted to grow. Then help her learn how to plant, tend, and harvest the produce or flowers. A nice touch might be to can or freeze some of the extras for winter use. Or you could make potpourri sachets from dried herbs and flowers. Discuss how God has made each plant unique

and how He designed each seed to carry all the information necessary to develop into a plant. Discuss the unique gifts God has given to you and your daughter. Ask Him to continue to develop these gifts.

3. **Dream about your "dream" house.** Encourage your daughter to plan her dream home. Keep a scrapbook of magazine pictures with special features she would like to include in her home someday. This would be a perfect time to discuss the importance of your heavenly home.

4. **Dream about traveling.** Plan a travel night. Get brochures and booklets from your local travel agency, or borrow books and videotapes from the library on a specific country you always have wanted to visit. Feature foods from this country. Check with a mission organization about the spiritual needs of the people in this country. Spend time in prayer, asking God to meet these needs.

5. **Dream about that perfect job.** Find a quiet time with your daughter to discuss the hopes and dreams you have for her. Talk about God-given attributes you've seen from the day she was born. Encourage her to consider how she can most effectively use her strengths. Ask your daughter to identify her dream job. Encourage her to talk to the school guidance counselor, take aptitude tests, investigate the possibilities for women in the workforce today,

and volunteer with organizations that special-
ize in fields that interest her. Remind your
daughter of the many ways to work directly for
the Lord and to witness her faith no matter
what her chosen occupation.

6. **Dream about relaxing times.** Have a tea party
with the special women in your life. Use your
best silverware and china and serve finger
sandwiches and fancy cookies. Arrange for a
baby-sitter and get rid of the guys so you can
relax and let the conversation—and the hot
tea—flow. Open the party with prayer, inviting
God to strengthen the ties of family and friend
relationships.

7. **Dream about your friendships.** Lie in the cool
grass or sit on a swing under the stars with your
daughter. Ask her to tell you about her best
friend and what makes that person so important. Discuss the qualities that an ideal friend
should possess. Then talk about what kind of a
friend each one of you are to the other and to
the people in your life. Remind each other that
Jesus, your Best Friend, is always with you.

8. **Dream about special moments.** Identify your
most enjoyable moments as a mother. Share
these with your daughter. Ask her to share the
things she likes best about your role in her life.
Ask her to describe the things she wants to do
and be as a mother. Take a day to share the
same conversation starters with your mother.

Thank her for the special memories you have
of her mothering. Collect these various
thoughts into a scrapbook to pass to the next
generations. Include a written prayer of thanks
to God for your mother and your daughter.

9. **Dream about wedding plans.** From childhood,
   most girls dream about falling in love and
   about their wedding day. Tell your daughter
   about your wedding. Ask her to describe her
   "storybook" wedding. Discuss qualities to look
   for in a future husband. Read Ephesians
   5:21–33 and discuss what the apostle Paul's
   statements mean for the Christian marriage.

10. **Dream about family resemblances.** Discuss
    physical features that your daughter has in
    common with other family members. Pull out
    the family photo albums and talk about the
    similarities. Emphasize what a creative God we
    have. Also emphasize His great love for us as
    demonstrated in His plan of salvation.
    Through Jesus' life, death, and resurrection, we
    are, by grace, members of God's family.

SURPRISES

Prayer

Heavenly Father,

Just as I love surprising my daughter with a brand-new dress or a cuddly stuffed toy, You love surprising me with gifts. Help me to recognize and rejoice in the surprises You plan for me: the first flower of spring, the last parking space when I'm rushed, a homemade card from my little one when I'm feeling down, or Your promise in a rainbow.

Teach my daughter to look for and recognize Your surprises too. Let her delight in them and thank You daily for the small gifts, as well as the big ones. Let her remember to look for the things You do for her unexpectedly, simply because she is Your child and You love her.

Help us, God, to trust You when the world throws surprises at us. When life puts a detour in our way, remind us that though life may not be certain, You are. Thank You for Your unchanging nature in the midst of surprises. In Jesus' name. Amen.

The "Keeper" of Surprises

Be alert and always keep on praying.
Ephesians 6:18

Katie was a beautiful 4-year-old with long hair the color of sunshine and eyes that rivaled the blue of a summer sky. While I was proud of everything about my daughter, I was especially proud of her hair. I suppose it was because I'd had hair like hers when I was younger, but it had turned a dull blonde over the years. Or perhaps it was because Katie had been born practically bald. I'd had to tape ribbons to her bare head so people would know she was a girl. Of course, for Katie, her hair couldn't have mattered less. Hair was hair, unless it belonged to her two teenaged sisters, Robin and Mary. She could spend hours watching them apply makeup and fix their hair.

One day, Earl took Katie to town. I didn't know what they were doing—he had said something about a surprise—but I didn't pay much attention as they left. When the car returned and Katie jumped out, I nearly fainted. Her wonderful hair that I had watched grow inch by inch had been cut above her shoulders. I couldn't believe it. Robin and Mary, who had walked into the room, saw my open mouth and unspoken horror. They grabbed Katie the moment she walked inside the house. Robin and Mary rushed her to her room and began "fixing" the unfixable. When they finished, she did look cute, but I already had convinced Earl that I did not want any more "surprises"—ever.

Of course, surprises come in all sizes, shapes, and varieties. Some are good; some are bad. We'd rather not deal with the bad surprises. We'd like time to prepare, to change, or to keep bad things from happening. That's not always possible. I could have kept the haircut from happening, if I'd known about it. It's better that we don't know about some surprises. We'd only worry and fret if we knew we were going to become ill or that the factory where we work would close.

Other surprises are always welcome. The unexpected promotion, the engagement ring, the long-anticipated baby. But we probably would find a way to confuse matters if we knew ahead of time about the good things. It's best if God is the "Keeper" of life's surprises.

There is, however, one surprise that God has planned for all His followers—Judgment Day. No, it's not a surprise that He's going to do it. He has been very up front about the fact that it will occur so we have time to prepare and spread the Gospel message. The surprise is the "when" of that day on which Jesus will return to earth to take His people home. God's Word says that no one knows the day or the time, but that we should remain alert.

That's good advice for daily living as well as for end-time living. Because Jesus came to suffer, die, and rise again to win our salvation, bad surprises can't overwhelm us. We know that we are God's children and even death can't defeat us. There are no truly bad surprises because God is on our side, protecting us, strengthening us, and preparing us. And by His Holy Spirit, we will be ready for the best surprise—Christ's second coming.

Lord, thank You that in Your mercy You provided for my eternal salvation. Help me to appreciate the surprises that come my way. Teach me to take them in stride, the good and the bad, and to make the most of each opportunity to serve You and witness to Your gracious love. In Jesus' name. Amen.

L.T.

Happy Mother's Day

*[Jesus] also saw a poor widow put in
two very small copper coins. "I tell you
the truth," He said, "this poor widow
has put in more than all the others. All
these people gave their gifts out of their
wealth; but she out of her poverty put in
all she had to live on." Luke 21:2–4*

It was the Saturday before Mother's Day. Jennifer had
spent the day with a friend at a local theme park. My 9-
year-old daughter arrived home carrying a paper bag, obviously from the restaurant where her friend's mother had
taken the girls to eat.

"Here, Mommy, this is for you!" Jennifer exclaimed as
she held out the bag.

"What is it?" I asked.

"It's an early Mother's Day present. I know how much
you like ice-cream sundaes, so I saved mine for you,"
Jennifer explained.

I took the bag from my daughter's hand. But as I held it,
I was surprised by how little it weighed. *How can there be
any ice cream inside?* I wondered.

Opening the bag, I looked inside and saw a container.
When I opened it, I discovered that less than half the original ice-cream sundae remained.

"Jennifer, I don't understand. It's almost gone," I said.

"I know," my daughter said matter-of-factly. "It was hard
not to eat it all, but I knew you would want some. So Happy

Mother's Day!" She hugged me and ran to get a spoon.

I sat down at the kitchen table. I must admit, the melted sundae didn't look appetizing. Jennifer had mixed the hot fudge into the vanilla ice cream, resulting in a particularly unattractive brownish tint. Alongside the swirled mess lay a droopy blob of whipped cream.

"See," Jennifer said proudly, pointing with the spoon, "I even saved you the cherry!" Sure enough, tucked under the melting mess was a red bulge.

"Thank you so much, Jennifer," I said sincerely. With each spoonful, I made lots of "ummm" sounds for my daughter's benefit.

While this may be hard to believe, Jennifer's ice-cream treat was the best sundae I've ever had. It wasn't much on looks, or even taste for that matter, but it was a gift of love.

Jennifer's gift reminded me of the story of the widow's mite. As Jesus sat near the place where the offerings were collected, He watched the crowd. As the rich threw large sums into the temple treasury, Jesus observed a poor widow leaving her offering. She put in two small copper coins, which were worth only a fraction of a penny.

Jesus explained to His disciples that the widow had given more than all the others. The rich gave out of their wealth, but she had given everything she had to live on, even though she was poor.

Like the widow, Jennifer had given a valuable gift. It was a sacrifice for her to save part of her sundae for me—the ultimate gift from someone who loves ice cream more than I do! Because of Jennifer's actions, I have come to look at people's gifts in a different light. I realize I may never know the sacrifice behind the gift. And as Jesus explained in the story of the widow's offering, generosity can't be measured by the value of the gift. Rather it is measured by the heart of the giver.

Lord Jesus, You gave me the most precious gift of forgiveness through Your sacrifice. Send Your Holy Spirit to lead me to follow Your example and truly give of myself—to my daughter, to my family, and to others. Amen.

N.O.B.

The Cross

*Be imitators of God, therefore, as dearly
loved children and live a life of love, just
as Christ loved us and gave Himself up
for us as a fragrant offering and sacrifice
to God. Ephesians 5:1–2*

Why do mothers try desperately to give evenly to their
children? I attempted to do this while my children were
growing up. Birthday presents, Christmas presents, souvenirs
from my travels—they all had to add up to the same amount
for each child. And this wasn't just a monetary balancing of
the scales—the gifts had to even out in appearance also.

Mary and Robin do the same thing with their children.
Every Christmas, they make lists and run around until the
last moment, making sure they have an equal amount of
gifts to distribute. From one birthday to the next, they must
remember who received what so the next child in line does-
n't feel slighted. The process gets to be quite a headache.

I thought I'd outgrown this because my children were
adults. I was wrong.

Several years ago, I attended a retreat at a Christian
retreat center. At the center's gift shop, I noticed a beautiful
cross pendant fashioned from gold and silver flowers. *It
would be so wonderful to buy each of my daughters a cross like
that,* I thought. It would be a family sign of unity and faith,
especially if they all had the same cross. It could become
something to pass down in their families.

There were two problems with my plan. First, I could

not afford to buy each daughter a cross at the same time. Second, the shop only had one cross. However, the shop-keeper assured me that the next time I was at the retreat center, she would have another in stock. "We try to keep one of each cross at all times," she said.

That's wonderful, I thought. *I can buy them for the girls one at a time.* The shopkeeper promised to reorder the same cross so I could purchase it when I was back in town. Because Katie was the only daughter still at home, and I had promised to bring her something, I bought the cross and gave it to her.

Katie loved it, and so did Mary and Robin. I was even more determined to establish the tradition of the flower cross for the women in our family. I would try to get one for each of us. Maybe I would even purchase one for each granddaughter.

For many reasons, I didn't return to the retreat center for two years. At the time of my visit, Robin had just been released from the hospital and needed something to keep up her spirits. I stopped at the gift shop to make my purchase. As promised, there was another cross exactly like Katie's. I paid for my purchase and told the shopkeeper that I would be back for another cross. I delivered my present to Robin.

Because my work continually took me in opposite direc-tions, I had to make a special trip to the retreat center to pick up Mary's cross. Since my last visit, though, the gift shop had been remodeled, the merchandise changed, and a new sales staff hired. The woman behind the counter had no idea what I was talking about when I said I wanted to buy another flower cross. She tried to be helpful and pulled out several merchandise books, but we couldn't find the cross.

"There is another manufacturer that they used to order from," she said. "I'll give you the number. Maybe you can order it directly."

I called the company and tried to describe to the representative the particular cross I wanted out of the more than 100 crosses she distributed. Finally, the woman asked me to photocopy the cross and send it to her so she could try to match the design.

And that's where I'm at now. If this woman can successfully identify the design, I intend to buy enough crosses for me, Mary, and for my granddaughters. Of course, Mary knows I love her with or without the cross. And I could have bought her something else—but I really wanted these crosses to be a special symbol of the bond between my daughters and me. I wanted to give them a reminder that both God and I will always love them and be with them.

Any mother will tell you that she loves all of her children the same, and that is true. But there is Someone who loves each of us more than anyone else in the world. Sounds impossible, doesn't it? But it's not—not when that Person is God. His love is not limited by time or space. He gave us what was most precious to Him—His Son—to fulfill His plan for our salvation. And Jesus went the greatest distance to prove His love—all the way to the cross, all the way to death in our place, all the way to victory on Easter morning.

Loving Lord, thank You for going to the cross for me. Help me to appreciate more fully how much You love me. Help me to tell others about Your unconditional, unending love so they might have life in abundance. Amen.

L.T.

But, Mom, Everyone's Wearing It

*"Come now, let us reason together," says
the LORD. Isaiah 1:18*

Jennifer and I were at the mall when she asked for some nail polish. As I surveyed the display of fashionable reds and pinks, Jennifer searched for a particular color she had in mind.

"Ah ha!" she exclaimed. "I found it."

I looked up to see her proudly holding a bottle of nail polish. "Isn't it great?" she announced, handing it to me.

"It's ... blue!" I said with a gasp of disbelief.

"Oh, come on, Mom, everyone's wearing it," Jennifer answered.

"*Blue* nail polish?" I said. "You've got to be kidding?"

Her hurt look told me she was quite serious about her selection. I thought it was entirely inappropriate for an 11-year-old. I gave her my "I don't care what everyone else is doing" speech, and we left the store without the nail polish.

Although Jennifer continued to ask for the blue nail polish, I stood my ground. There was no way I wanted to see blue, purple, or green polish on my young lady's nails. She wasn't "that kind of girl."

About two weeks later, Jennifer spent the night at her friend Kimberly's house.

When Jennifer came home the next day, she ran up and held out her hands. "Look what Kimberly did!" she announced. On each nail Kimberly meticulously had painted a dainty *blue* daisy. Over each flower, she'd brushed a glittery see-through topcoat, which gave Jennifer's nails a stylish, professional look. The effect wasn't gaudy or off-the-wall. I also knew that if Jennifer had this done at a nail salon, I'd have spent a small fortune for this trendy work of art.

"Jennifer, they're beautiful!" I exclaimed as I held her hands in mine. She smiled, then ran off to call a girlfriend.

Later I asked God if I had been wrong to say she couldn't get the blue nail polish. The light blue she'd selected was what Kimberly had used to paint the delicate daisies on Jennifer's nails. I decided to make an effort to notice what color polish "everyone else" was wearing at school. During the following weeks, I saw every color imaginable painted on teenage girls' nails. After seeing some pretty outrageous colors and "paint jobs," I decided that my daughter's plea for a demure, tasteful light blue wasn't such an extreme request after all.

Sometimes my preconceived notions about things or people get me into trouble. I confess that I don't always think before I speak. In the case of the blue polish, I'm guilty of making a quick decision without having all the facts.

God's Word tells us to consider carefully what we do (2 Chronicles 19:6). Not only do I need an open mind when contemplating a decision, but I need to seek God's guidance as well. After all, if He had made a snap judgment about me, He would have seen a sinner and left me to my punishment. But God saw a solution to the problem of sin and sent Jesus as my Savior. He came in God's perfect time to be the final answer to the problem of sin, death, and the devil.

As my daughter continues to grow and mature, I will be faced with more difficult decisions than approving a nail polish color. I pray that God will continue to lead me as I look to Him for the ability to make wise decisions.

O God of wisdom and truth, open my eyes to Your desires before I open my mouth to others. Forgive my snap judgments and incorrect decisions. Give me patience and insight as I interact with my daughter. In Jesus' name. Amen.

N.O.B.

God's Triple-A Service

*Jesus had compassion on them and
touched their eyes. Immediately they
received their sight and followed Him.
Matthew 20:34*

Katie and I were on our way home from a writers' con-
ference on St. Simons Island, Georgia, when she asked if we
could stop at a shopping mall we had passed on the way
down. "It'll be a good place to get something to eat," she
said. "And it will give us an opportunity to get out of the
van for a few minutes." She stretched and looked sheepishly
at me.

"It would also be a good place to look for a new pair of
jeans," I said with a laugh. Katie smiled back. She knew I
really didn't mind. I like malls as much as she does. We
parked, locked the doors, and walked to a small restaurant
that was part of the complex. After the 90-degree tempera-
tures outside, it was nice to be inside the air-conditioned
building. After lunch, we strolled through several stores,
bought a pair of jeans and a T-shirt, and returned to the
van.

As we put our purchases away, we noticed that something was wrong with one of the tires. A big knot was
bulging from the tread. "We can't drive with a tire like
that," I said. We both stared at the back of the van, which
was loaded with a week's worth of clothes, boxes of books
and teaching materials, souvenirs, beach chairs, and more.

The spare tire and the jack were beneath everything.

"We can't change the tire," Katie asserted. I had changed a tire before but on a car, not the van. Katie and I didn't even know where to put the jack.

"We'd better call AAA," I told Katie, digging in my purse for the card. We'd been members for years but hadn't used the service often. Within an hour, a pleasant young man arrived in a large truck, moved our luggage, removed the tire and jack, changed the tire, replaced everything, and all I had to do was sign the receipt.

"That's the best deal I've ever seen," Katie said as we climbed in the van to continue our journey. "Where can I sign up?"

"You're already signed up," I told her, "because you're a member of our family."

I thought about that incident as we drove toward North Carolina. God is like AAA service for Christians. He removes the excess baggage of sin, takes care of us in emergencies, and keeps us moving on the path of life. But He's much better than AAA. We don't have to pay a thing for God's services—there's no annual membership. In fact, He sent His only Son to pay the price for our participation in His family. Jesus' suffering and death cancel the debt of our sin. His resurrection assures us of our place in heaven forever.

The question is, do we treat God like AAA? Do we only call when there's a problem, even though we have the privilege of being with our heavenly Father every day in His Word and sacraments?

Dear Lord, thank You for giving me a free membership in Your salvation plan through Jesus, my Savior. Remind me that I can call You during times of emergency and times of peace. Thank You for Your faithfulness to me. Keep me faithful to You and to those You've asked me to serve. In Jesus' name. Amen.

L.T.

Just Desserts

I can do all things through Christ which strengtheneth me. Philippians 4:13 (KJV)

I had been enjoying a delightful lunch with my friend Kathy when our waitress asked if we wanted dessert. "Yes, I'd like to have the homemade peach cobbler, warmed, with a scoop of vanilla ice cream," she answered immediately. Then Kathy turned to me and asked, "How about you?"

"Sounds good to me," I said.

When the waitress left, however, I silently scolded myself. Now in my fourth decade, my metabolism has unfairly slowed down, and it is far too easy to put on extra pounds. A few minutes later, our desserts arrived. Although the cobbler was scrumptious, I couldn't enjoy it because of the guilt I felt for my lack of self-control.

The following week I looked through my closet. I had great hopes of finding a pair of slacks that were big enough to allow me to breathe after zipping them. It was obvious that too many cookies and peach cobblers had taken their toll.

As I shimmied a pair of slacks up my legs, Jennifer walked into my bedroom. "What are you doing with all those clothes on your bed?" she asked.

"I'm trying to find something that fits." I plopped down beside her and lamented my weight gain.

My 10-year-old listened sympathetically, then said, "That's okay, Mommy. I love you whether you're skinny or fat." She kissed me and left the room.

Fat? Does she think I'm fat? I wondered. *I've only got to lose about 15 ... well, maybe 20 pounds.*

Over the next few weeks, I tried to shed the extra weight through diets and walking. I only lost a few pounds and gained them back in no time. Disgusted and frustrated, my self-esteem plummeted.

Jennifer noticed that I was feeling particularly low. After church she handed me an index card. "Here, Mommy, this is for you." Her eager expression told me it was a special note. On it she had drawn a picture of the two of us with smiling faces. Underneath she had written something I'd forgotten about during the past six months: *You are beautiful in His sight!*

Jennifer's card still sits on my window sill. It serves as a constant reminder that my precious Lord loves me for who I am. He would have come to earth to save me, even if I were the only person here. I am His special daughter. And He has given me a special daughter to love and who loves me.

Lord, remind me constantly of how precious I am to You. Help me to communicate to my daughter the importance You have in my life and in hers. Amen.

N.O.B.

A Peace that Passes All Understanding

I will lie down and sleep in peace, for You alone, O LORD, make me dwell in safety. Psalm 4:8

Mary was a teenager when she made her first trip to New York City with me. I was going for a staff meeting at a magazine, and she was going because I had begged her to come. I thought it would be a treat for her, and she thought it was torture.

It wasn't that Mary didn't want to go to the Big Apple. She didn't want to fly. If Mary could have traveled in a car, train, or bus, she would have been thrilled. Because she has always been a bit claustrophobic, being cooped up in an airplane thousands of feet in the air wasn't exactly her idea of a vacation.

Mary finally consented to go. I promised that God would take care of us as He always did. "He doesn't mind flying on airplanes," I said. "In fact, He likes high places!" I was fairly successful at keeping her mind on other matters while we were in the air, though she did cover her eyes several times with my eye shades. She might have fooled the other passengers, but I knew she wasn't asleep. She was trying to avoid where she was.

We landed safely and survived the cab ride to Manhattan. I could almost hear her sigh of relief when we walked into our room. Mary threw her bag on the bed and headed for the bathroom—something she never would have done on the airplane and hadn't had time for at the airport. A few minutes later, I heard her turn the doorknob. I finished putting my things away and turned to ask if she wanted to go out for a while, but Mary wasn't there. "Mary," I called. "Where are you?"

"I'm in here! I can't get the door open," she yelled from the bathroom. She tried to turn the handle, but it wouldn't budge. "What am I going to do?" Her voice was panicky. "It's locked! It won't open. Do something!"

It was hard to believe that Mary had flown safely here only to become stuck in a hotel bathroom hardly big enough to hold one person.

"Hang on," I said, after trying the door myself. "I'll call maintenance." I dialed the hotel switchboard and explained that my daughter was locked in the bathroom. Then I sat down outside the bathroom door and talked to Mary while we waited for someone to come.

At times, I had to suppress my urge to laugh—the whole situation was so comical. But I knew I didn't dare laugh—it was extremely serious to Mary. She may be able to breeze through rush hour traffic in the biggest city or swim like a fish or stand before a crowd to sing a solo, but tell Mary that she will be confined in a tiny bathroom on the 24th floor of a Manhattan hotel for an hour, and you've got a real problem.

That's why I was impressed that she kept her cool while the maintenance man removed the door. When she finally emerged, she did so with dignity and sense of humor intact. "How did you handle it so well?" I asked her.

"Well," she hesitated before continuing, "if God likes airplanes, I decided He probably liked too-small bathrooms too. And I figured if He could get me off that plane, He could surely get me out of that bathroom."

Mary enjoyed the rest of the trip, but I believe she'll never be the first one in a strange bathroom again!

We all have personal fears, things that cause us to freeze and become unable to function normally. Only the Lord can help us defeat our fears. He invites us to place our trust in Him that He will see us through the difficulties of life.

God has even removed the biggest fear from our lives. Because of Christ's suffering, death, and resurrection, we don't have to fear punishment for our sins. Christ took that punishment for us and gave us the freedom of being God's beloved daughters. We know exactly what will happen when we die. We will go to live with God forever. That means we can sleep in peace, fly in peace, and enter tight places in peace because God is by our side.

Father, thank You for Your presence in every moment of my life—from times of fear to times of rejoicing, from the deepest valleys to the highest mountaintops. Thank You for removing all fear of punishment and death through the saving work of Your Son. Help me to share the joy of Your peace and salvation with my daughter. Amen.

L.T.

Who's Going to Be God?

I will walk among you and be your God,
and you will be My people.
Leviticus 26:12

The lights on our Christmas tree twinkled as I guided a red ribbon around the present I was wrapping. Humming along with the holiday music, I noticed Jennifer admiring our nativity scene. Carefully picking up the porcelain figurine of Mary, she asked, "Mom, who's gonna play the part of Mary in the Christmas pageant?"

"Amberly is going to be Mary," I answered.

Replacing the figurine in the stable, she inquired, "Who will be the shepherds?"

As I answered her questions, we talked about each of my students and the role they would play in the annual Christmas pageant.

Finally, Jennifer asked, "Well, who's gonna be God?"

I chuckled at her question. As I continued to reflect on it, a small voice stirred inside me, asking, *Who's going to be God in your life, Nancy?*

Sometimes I'm guilty of trying to play God. I turn a problem over to God only to take it back again. Impatient for an answer, I think I can handle things better or faster.

But God has the answer for my impatience—His Son. In God's own time, He sent Jesus to earth. Jesus lived the perfect, patient life I can't live. Then He completed God's plan for my salvation by dying on the cross. Through faith in Him, I have forgiveness for my lack of patience and the assurance of a future life in heaven.

Through the power of the Holy Spirit, it is my role to rely on God for all things. It is my role to trust God for the answers. Then I won't have to ask myself, *Who's going to be God?* I'll already know.

Father, help me to leave my burdens at Your feet.
Grant me the patience to wait on Your perfect timing
for the answers to my questions. In my Savior's name.
Amen.

N.O.B.

Emergency Surgery

Now choose life, so that you and your
children may live and that you may love
the LORD your God, listen to His voice,
and hold fast to Him. For the LORD is
your life. Deuteronomy 30:19b–20a

Evelyn and I were friends from the first time we met. We shared a yard in the housing project where we lived as teenagers. We also shared clothes, homework, and secrets. She was everything I ever wanted in a friend. We were the same age—in fact our birthdays were only a few days apart. We were so alike that she knew what I was thinking before I said it. Evelyn also taught me that to live life did not mean to exist from day to day.

I would have done anything for Evelyn, but I couldn't take away the cancer that eventually took her life. She was in her late 20s when she learned about the cancer. She had three daughters and a loving husband. It was a matter of weeks from the diagnosis to the day she died. I couldn't understand why I was blessed by God to still be with my girls while she had to leave her daughters motherless.

I was in my late 40s when I understood how truly blessed I was. I had had several minor surgeries during my life but nothing serious. I had gone to the doctor because of a possible hernia from a previous surgery. I expected to need some type of repair, but I believed it would be minor surgery. I wasn't worried.

The doctor sent me to the hospital for some x-rays. The

radiologist who read my x-rays noticed something suspicious. Following more tests, my gynecologist told me there was a tumor and I would need surgery in two days. "We're not sure, but it looks and feels like it might be on your ovary," he said.

I didn't know at the time how serious ovarian cancer is. The doctors knew, the radiologist knew, and my daughter Robin knew. Through her work at the hospital, Robin had met many women who came in for routine checkups and died within a few months. Of course, she didn't tell me this when I called her. She quietly said, "I'll be there tomorrow night so I can be with you when you go to the hospital."

I was pleased that Robin was coming, of course, and that Mary had changed her work schedule to be at the hospital when we arrived. I was even surprised at how easy it was to get Katie and Andy out of bed that morning. As we drove to the hospital, they were unusually quiet. I tried making small talk, but I was getting nervous. Until that point, I had barely had time to think. I put things in order at home, completed a writing project, and prepared meals for the family. All in two days.

On the drive to the hospital, though, I began to think of Evelyn. They had found a growth in her breast, and she had died a few short months later. As we walked to the entrance of the hospital and approached Mary, I looked at my children. *Sometimes I take important things for granted*, I thought. I had seen my children through grade school, high school, college, marriage, babies, and many other milestones. Evelyn had not had that privilege.

I don't know what happened during the hours I was on the operating table. I do remember being prepared for surgery, taking some relaxation medication, and telling my family that I loved them. Sometime later, I heard the doctor calling my name. "Linda," he said. "Linda, wake up. Linda, can you hear me?"

"Yes," I said, trying to focus my eyes on my doctor. "Yes, I hear you." I saw him standing above me, then I shut my eyes against the glare of the lights.

"I just wanted to tell you that the growth was not malignant! We got it all, and it was benign," he said. "I wanted to give you the news myself." I opened my eyes to see a grin spread across his face. "And I also wanted to tell you that you've got a group of children out there who really love you. I wish you could have heard them when I told them it wasn't cancer!"

"Yes, I do, don't I?" I mumbled as he patted me on the shoulder and turned to leave.

I learned later that none of them had left the waiting room during the operation. They asked intelligent, well-informed questions. They made plans on who would stay with me each night and what they would do when I got home. And they offered a prayer of thanksgiving when the doctor told them I'd be fine.

But Evelyn had great kids too. Why some of us are taken so young and others are granted the privilege of seeing their children grow up, I don't know. What I do know is that we have a great God. He provides answers for the things we need to know. He provides the answer for our salvation through Jesus Christ. He provides faithful family and friends who love us. And He provided me with a friend who taught me to live life more fully—through her life as well as her death.

Father, thank You for giving me courage and strength when I am weak and for overcoming sin and death once for all. Thank You for the hope I have in my resurrected Savior, who has prepared a place for me in heaven. Help me celebrate my victory in Jesus who left behind Him an empty cross and empty tomb. In His name I pray. Amen.

L.T.

Dance with Me

You turned my wailing into dancing; ...
and clothed me with joy. Psalm 30:11

Jennifer has always loved to dance. I can remember her
first "dance" vividly. She was almost 2 years old and was
playing in the family room. A television commercial began
blaring a catchy song. Jennifer stopped what she was doing
and began swaying to the music. She was transfixed.

As the music continued, my little girl lifted her arms
and moved her hands up and down. A smile crept across her
face and her eyes lit up. When the music stopped, so did
she. Just as naturally as her dance had begun, she returned
to her task. At that moment I knew that Jennifer's love of
dance would tiptoe repeatedly into our lives.

When Jennifer turned 3, I enrolled her in a toddler
dance class. She looked adorable in her pink leotard, tights,
and ballet slippers! My pint-sized ballerina looked forward
to the lessons and caught on quickly. She was a natural.

As the years passed, Jennifer became a talented dancer.
Her poise and beauty now hold *me* transfixed as I watch her
gracefully dance at ballet recitals or to any music she plays.

One day, I was listening to a Christian tape while
preparing dinner. Although its words beckoned me to relax,
my mind wandered to the list of chores that already exceed-
ed the number of hours in my day. Totally engrossed in the
"to dos," I was unaware that Jennifer *had* noticed the music
and was already dancing.

"Isn't it beautiful?" I finally heard her say. It was the
kind of song that makes you want to move to the rhythm.

"Mommy, come dance with me," my daughter solicited. She took me by the hand and led me to the living room. As Christian singer Lori Wilke sang of God's love, I felt my mind, body, and soul relax. I stood for a moment and watched Jennifer praise the Lord with her dancing. With her back arched and her head and eyes to the heavens, she elegantly raised her arms in a position of praise and adoration. Then in one graceful move, she glided over to me and took both of my hands.

My daughter looked deeply into my eyes—right into the part reserved for wishing. Oh, how I wished I could dance like my daughter! I longed to move as elegantly as she did, to be so totally caught up in the music that you had to dance to express who you are and what you're all about.

As I gazed into her eyes, I saw such love and happiness that my feet began to move. I was as entranced as she was as we twirled around the living room. I felt so free! Free from cares and deadlines. Free from a demanding list of chores. And best of all, free to enjoy the music and to dance for joy.

The moment was timeless. I realized that I didn't have to be a gifted dancer like my daughter. All I needed to be was willing—willing to leave my cares and duties behind. Willing to come dance when the Lord beckoned and to be filled with His joy. And what joy He gives! I only need to think of that first Christmas night, when the angels sang for joy because God had sent the promised Savior to redeem the world, including me.

Now I don't wait for Jennifer to ask me to dance. As soon as my favorite song comes on, I extend my hand and ask her to dance with me.

Heavenly Father, remind me that my day is never too busy and that now is a good time to dance! Amen.

N.O.B.

The Perfect Neighbor

*So he asked Jesus, "And who is my
neighbor?" Luke 10:29b*

Some people complain about their neighbors, but I love
mine. They make it easy to follow Jesus' command to "love
your neighbor as yourself." This could be because one of
them is my daughter Mary and the other is my daughter-in-
law, Christy.

We weren't sure how well we would get along when
Mary and her family moved into a mobile home in a wood-
ed area about half a mile from us. Then Andy and Christy
moved into a trailer on the spot where our farm's original
homestead had been. Our driveway passes Andy and
Christy's home, and we can watch Mary's children play from
our front porch.

These living arrangements have worked because we
have tried to head off any problems. Each of us calls the
other before visiting to see if it's a good time to drop in. The
grandchildren ask permission before showing up at our door.
Nobody borrows anything without asking first. One of the
families takes care of our house and animals when we travel,
and we baby-sit when the sitter is sick. There's always a car
to use if one breaks down, and everyone comes to our house
if a snowstorm cuts off the electricity to the trailers. There's
something warm and cozy, safe and reassuring about having
such wonderful neighbors.

But what if my neighbors weren't members of my family? Would I love them then? Jesus says anyone can love people who love them (Matthew 5:46–47), but He calls us to a higher standard: to love even our enemies. After all, we were God's enemies and He loved us enough to send Jesus to give His life for us (Romans 5:6–11). Through the power of the Holy Spirit, we can love those around us—family, friends, neighbors, and even strangers.

Blessed Redeemer, I praise You for loving Your enemies—including me—and for dying and rising again for us. Help me to love and serve those who are hard to love. Help me to see their desperate need for a Savior and to share the Good News with them. Thank You for love that frees and knows no end. Amen.

L.T.

Wrapped in Love

I will not forget you! See, I have
engraved you on the palms of My hands.
Isaiah 49:15b–16a

I stood at the kitchen counter making sandwiches for my children's school lunches. In my mind I replayed what my first-grader, Jennifer, had said earlier.

"Mommy, do you miss me when I'm at school?"

"Sure I miss you," I answered.

"I miss you a lot, and I wish you could be there to tell me how much you love me," Jennifer said.

Wrapping her sandwich in plastic wrap, I wondered how I could remind my little girl that I thought about her and that I loved her, even while we were apart.

I wrote Jennifer's name on a strip of masking tape and put it on her sandwich. An idea hit me. I could write a "love note" and tape it to her sandwich. When she took her sandwich out of her lunch box, she would be reminded of me and of my love for her.

I ripped off another strip of tape and wrote: "I love you. See you soon! Love, Mommy."

The next morning I packed the lunch boxes and sent Jennifer and Matthew off to school. She hadn't seen the note, so I knew it would be a surprise.

When I picked Jennifer up that afternoon, she was grinning from ear to ear. Climbing into the front seat, she leaned over and hugged me. "I love you too," she said.

Over the years I've changed my messages to fit the occasion. When Jennifer has been concerned about a test, phrases such as "I know you can do it!" or "I'm praying for you" adorn her sandwich. I've even decorated the tape with smiley faces and hearts and written notes on colored paper cut in the shape of a heart. Just as long as my daughter knows I'm thinking of her, it doesn't matter how the message is expressed.

Isn't it amazing what those three little words can do for someone? The assurance it gave my 5-year-old was priceless. She knew that no matter where she was, she was on my mind. And I know that when she's grown and leaves home, I'll still think of her daily. I know that my mother still thinks about me.

It's nice to know that someone is thinking about us. And it's especially nice to know that God always has His beloved ones on His heart and mind. The Bible tells us that we are wrapped in the protection of His love. The great I Am declares that He loves us with an everlasting love. He has demonstrated that love through the saving work of His Son. His "love notes" are written upon our hearts and our very name is engraved upon the palm of His hands. We can be assured that we will never be forgotten.

Devoted God, I'm so grateful that You love me with an everlasting love. Thank You for showing me the extent of Your love at the cross and the empty tomb. Help me reach out to others with the power of Your saving Word. Let my words and actions express love. In Jesus' name. Amen.

N.O.B.

Through the Faith of a Child

" 'If You can'?" said Jesus. "Everything
is possible for him who believes."
Mark 9:23

The snow started falling sometime during the night. An early, unexpected December snow—something we were unaccustomed to in North Carolina. Most of our snows come in January and February, if they come at all. We're surrounded by mountains that protect us from most of the bad weather.

But whoever said snow was bad? Not my grandchildren. They donned coats, hats, and gloves; fastened plastic bags over their shoes; and went out to play. It snowed all day, and they played all day. They stayed outside until they were nearly frozen. Then they bounded into the house to warm up before they went outside again. On their last trip into the house, Mary warned them, "If you don't stop dragging in snow, I'm going to take a big fan outside and blow those snow clouds away. Then we'll turn the heater up high, open the doors, and melt what's already there."

The older kids just laughed, but her youngest, Marcus, looked like he was going to cry. "Oh no, Mama," he cried. "Please don't do that, I'll wipe my shoes off next time, I promise!"

We could all learn a lesson from this young child who truly believed his mother could blow the clouds away and melt the snow. Jesus tells us that everything is possible with

God—of course, He wasn't talking about stopping a snow-storm. At least, not the way Mary had pronounced she would do it.

Why is it that faith becomes more difficult as we grow older? Is it because we become jaded to the work of our heavenly Father? Do we become complacent in our desire to be in His presence through Word and sacrament? Do we falter because we have seen things that didn't go our way or give up when the prayed-for answer doesn't arrive quickly enough?

Reading God's Word puts us in touch with the source of our faith—God Himself. He is at work through the power of His Word to strengthen our trust in Him and our faith in His promises. As we cling to God's Word, we see Him at work in our lives, deepening our understanding of His ways, bringing forth spiritual fruit in our lives, and encouraging the child-like faith that trusts our heavenly Father.

Dear Lord, thank You for giving me faith through the Holy Spirit in Your Son, Jesus, who loved me, died for me, and rose from the grave for me. Deepen my faith so I may bear fruit and cling to Your truth. Help me become like a little child in my faith. In my Savior's name. Amen.

L.T.

Only Human

My grace is sufficient for you, for My
power is made perfect in weakness.
2 Corinthians 12:9

I awoke to a melody of birds singing outside my bedroom window. Rolling to my side, I pulled the sheet up to
my chin. The house was peaceful and my bed cozy. I inhaled
deeply and lazily opened one eye to peer at the clock.

Oh no, it can't be nine o'clock! my mind screamed as
panic slapped me wide awake. I bolted from my bed and
dashed to Jennifer's bedroom.

"Wake up, Jennifer!" I commanded as I shook her by
the shoulder. "Mommy overslept." I opened her blinds to
allow the morning sun to flood her room with light. "You
have to hurry or you'll be late for summer rec."

My sleepy 7-year-old groaned from her bed. Hurrying
had never been her style. In fact, she was always the one
whom I had to wake up early so she had plenty of time to
get moving.

After making sure Jennifer was awake, I went back to
my room to shower and dress. I applied some makeup in
record time, then hurried to the kitchen to get my daughter
something to eat.

"Come on, Jen, let's go!" I hollered like a marine drill
sergeant. She plopped down onto a chair while I poured
some milk over a small bowl of cereal. "Eat!" I commanded
while I quickly brushed her hair and pulled it into a ponytail.

Between bites she asked, "Mommy, why didn't you set your alarm?"

"I did," I answered.

"Why didn't you get up?" she asked incredulously.

"I was tired. I fell back asleep." We talked for a while longer, but no matter how I explained it, Jennifer couldn't understand that I just didn't automatically get up in the morning. She couldn't conceive of the notion that her mother could make such a huge mistake. I'd fallen from the pedestal on which my young daughter had placed me. She realized that I'm not perfect and she even had proof!

Her apparent surprise made me think about how she perceives me. As her mother, Jennifer thinks I have all the answers. She feels secure in knowing I am wiser than she is and able to protect and guide her.

But since that crazy morning, I've made it a point to let Jennifer know that I am human and that I do make mistakes. (And there have been plenty of opportunities to reinforce that message!) I want my daughter to know that it's okay to try something new, even though there's no guarantee for success.

When I've been cranky and have said something unkind to Jennifer, I've apologized and asked for her forgiveness. This has taught her the importance of confession and repentance.

When I'm not sure of something, I've told Jennifer that I don't know. In some instances, we've looked for the answer together. Other times we've prayed for wisdom and have waited for the Lord to guide us.

Jennifer is in middle school now and knows full well that her family and friends aren't perfect. But over the years, she's learned that there is Someone who is perfect and who has all the answers. During her times of crisis, she turns to the God who created her and saved her. She has trusted Him for the solutions. Relying on her heavenly Father, she's learned firsthand that in our weakness, He is our strength. And knowing that to be true, each one of us can be content to be "only human."

> *Lord Jesus, thank You for loving me even though I make mistakes and fail You in multiple ways. Thank You for Your saving work at the cross on my behalf. Encourage me daily to become more like You, and forgive me when I fall short of the mark. Amen.*

N.O.B.

Love Knots

~tie your love together with these ideas

Surprise Each Other

1. **"Girls Only" surprise.** Have a pajama party. Little girls can pick out a favorite book or movie for entertainment. Older daughters could introduce you to their music. Grandmother or mother can bring a card game from her childhood such as pinochle, bridge, or gin rummy. Plan to giggle a lot. Each of you also can bring a favorite Bible verse or story and relate a time when you saw God at work in your life.

2. **Dramatic surprise.** Put together a drama or puppet show or lead a sing-along at a local nursing home. This would be memorable for the residents of the home as well as for you and your daughter or mother. If possible, use a Bible story as the basis for the drama or include familiar hymns or childhood "Jesus" songs.

3. **Scrapbook surprise.** Gather all those awards, special recognitions, programs, and favorite photos you've thrown into a drawer. Surprise your mother or daughter by arranging them in a scrapbook. Add captions and dates. Perhaps you'll want to add your own love letter.

Include appropriate Bible passages that will remind your loved one of the relationship you share as daughters of the heavenly Father.

4. **Rainy day surprise.** Gather materials and instructions for learning a new craft and spring it on your daughter as a special surprise on a dull, rainy, stay-inside day. Or call your mother long-distance just to talk. You could even make it a three-generation call, if possible. You also might keep a rainy-day box full of Christian videos, fiction, picture books, craft and activity books, etc. After all, rainy days are perfect days to curl up with the Good Book.

5. **Gift surprise.** Give your daughter or mother a gift for no reason except to show your love. This can be as simple as a card (homemade or store-bought), a plate of cookies or brownies, or a bouquet of flowers from your garden. Be creative.

6. **Outdoor surprise.** Go hiking together and/or plan an overnight camping trip complete with a campfire, marshmallows, and sleeping bags. For the less adventuresome, plan a picnic in the backyard. Include a Bible study or devotion that focuses on God and His creation.

7. **Treasure hunt surprise.** Work together as mother and daughter to plan a treasure hunt for the rest of the family. Write clues on slips of paper. (The first clue might be something like: "Swing high, swing low. You'll find the next clue directly below." The next clue, of course, would be under the swing.) One clue leads to

the next until the treasure is found. Celebrate your success as a family.

8. **Favorite guest surprise.** Invite your daughter's favorite teacher, coach, or pastor to dinner. Read a book about etiquette with your daughter ahead of time. Teach her how to properly set the table and the best way to greet her guest and make him or her feel comfortable. Help her to understand that good manners are always important. Encourage her to identify simple ways to witness to her faith in Jesus, especially if the guest is not a Christian.

9. **Let-her-decide surprise.** Take a day off from work or everyday household duties to spend time with your daughter or mother. Let her decide what the two of you will do. At the end of the day, thank God together for time with each other.

10. **Makeover surprise.** Surprise your daughter with a "makeover" day. For your teenager, gather eye shadow, blush, lipstick, nail polish, and any hair products that will be needed. Spend an hour or so experimenting with different hairstyles and teaching your daughter the proper application of each beauty product. For an older daughter or for your mother, schedule an appointment for the two of you at a local beauty salon to have a professional makeover. Compliment each other on the beautiful traits God has given you. Thank Him for these as well.

CHALLENGES

Prayer

Heavenly Father,

Reach out to my daughter and me. Remind us to join hands to face the challenges of the day. Let us feel the strength of Your nurturing hand covering our clasped ones, tightening our bond.

Renew our hearts and minds. Keep us from becoming self-seeking in a self-centered world. Give us a new heart and new spirit as You have promised.

Rescue us from ourselves. Make right our wrongs—the hasty words, the thoughtless actions. Give us the courage to examine ourselves, recognize our weaknesses, and make the most of our strengths.

Restore us to fellowship with You and others. Help us to love those who may not love us in return and to be kind to those who are unkind to us. Empower us with Your Holy Spirit so our lives may bring glory to Your name. In Jesus' name. Amen.

Star Wars

*"Your Father knows what you need
before you ask Him." Matthew 6:8*

Ahhh, the adolescent years. Have you started this roller
coaster ride yet? Perhaps you're a lucky mom who has survived and your daughter is beyond these hormonally imbal-
anced years. If you are in this position, you'll understand my
story.

The day began innocently. It was Friday and school was
out for the summer. The only thing on the day's agenda was
to get Jennifer's clothing and toiletries together for a week
at church camp.

We were both excited. This would be my daughter's first
time away from home and her first time at camp. Since the
week would be filled with crafts and outdoor activities, I
cautioned Jennifer not to bring her new or favorite clothes.

"But, Mom, I don't want to look like a loser," was her
retort.

I could see that this would be no simple packing job. It
was turning into another one of "life's little challenges."

"Jennifer, I'm not asking you to bring anything that
doesn't fit or that isn't stylish. All you need is shorts and T-
shirts—nothing fancy," I explained.

"But I don't have any decent shirts," she answered.

I could feel my jaw tighten and my teeth clench. We'd
gone shopping recently, and as far as I was concerned, she
had plenty of options. I walked to her closet and pulled out

a pair of shorts and a T-shirt. "Here you go. This looks nice together," I said as I proudly held the two pieces of clothing against each other.

"Yeah, right," Jennifer replied as she rolled her eyes.

"What's wrong with this?" I asked in total disbelief that my selection wasn't fashionable for camp life in the '90s.

"I won't wear that. It makes me look fat," was the answer.

"But you're not fat, so how could you look fat? Okay, how about this shirt then?" I questioned, pulling another T-shirt from her closet.

"Noooo! That's not in style."

By then I'd had it. "Jennifer Marie Boffo!" I yelled. "There's nothing wrong with these clothes. What's the matter with you? Do you think you have to be dressed like a star?"

Her "look" told me that's exactly what she thought. I told her to pick out her own clothing and I'd be back later to check her selections.

Besides the above conversation, other ugly things had been said. In my anger, I'd managed to say the very things I promised never to say as a parent. And as I wallowed in my guilt and misery, that's when I heard the still small voice of God.

Deep within, I remembered how my brilliant decisions hadn't turned out the way I'd hoped. But throughout my "growing pains," my faithful Father had loved me—patiently, unconditionally, and without condemnation. He had sent Christ to earth to repair the breach my self-absorption and sin had caused. And now He was making it clear to me that, with His help, I could do the same for my daughter.

I returned to Jennifer's bedroom. Although she stood in front of me with her arms crossed and her eyes avoiding me, I spoke. Softly, I told her that I was sorry and asked her to forgive me. "We'll figure this out together, okay?" I said.

With tears in her eyes, she hugged me, then looked at me. "I forgive you, Mommy, and will you forgive me?"

After assuring my precious daughter that I had already done so, we walked to her closet and began to look for something that would allow my daughter to feel like the shining star I knew she was.

O Father God, help me recognize the moments when I need to compromise with my daughter and work with her instead of against her. Thank You for the saving grace that has made me Your loved child. Help me to demonstrate to others the same unconditional love You show to me through Jesus, my Savior. In His name. Amen.

N.O.B.

Meeting the Challenges of Everyday Life

Love the LORD your God with all your
heart and with all your soul and with all
your strength. These commandments that
I give you today are to be upon your
hearts. Impress them on your children.
Deuteronomy 6:5–7

It seemed strange that I made my living using and editing words, but I could not come up with any to tell my children what they meant to me. I didn't know how to get the message across without sounding "mushy." As youngsters they wouldn't stand still long enough to listen to a sentimental Mom. They were more interested in running outside to play with the neighborhood children. The teenage years were even worse. "Oh, Mother, not now!" they'd say as they dialed a telephone number or hunted for car keys. And now that they are adults with busy lives of their own, how could I get them to listen to what I desperately wanted to say?

Then I thought of the letters my mother and I used to write to each other. They didn't start out as expressions of love. In fact, the first one evolved because my mother didn't know how else to reach me. I was 11 and decided I was in love with an older man, a 14-year-old to be exact. Instead of listening to her advice, I creatively came up with numerous ways to see him, even though I wasn't allowed to date at the time.

That was my first mistake. My second mistake was to write a long letter to my best friend that described an elaborate relationship with this boy that existed mostly in my mind. And the third mistake was leaving my letter lying on my bed. Of course it fell open when my mother straightened the covers.

When I went into my room after school, there was a letter waiting for me—from my mother. In this letter she expressed her disappointment in my behavior. She told me that I would be grounded for the next month. Of course, I expected punishment after I saw my letter lying beside hers, but I didn't expect the conclusion to her letter. She wrote that we would never mention this again because she trusted me not to do anything like it again.

And I didn't. Not because my secrets had been found out. Not because I was punished. But because she had such faith in me.

Over the next three years, my mother and I found that the letters worked for us. Either of us could safely say whatever we wanted without fear of being interrupted or misinterpreted by the other. And we had time to think about an answer before responding.

I was about 14 when I wrote to her about another young man. We were living on an air force base in Alaska, and I was allowed to date—as long as it wasn't one of the servicemen. Of course, I hated to be around all those attractive young men in uniform, with few girls to vie for their attention, and not be able to go out with any of them.

I became even unhappier about the situation when I met a young airman who worked in the base cafeteria. Over several weeks, we became friends as he served me sodas or fixed special order hamburgers for me. I learned that he was only 15 years old. His mother had signed so he could enter the service. Because he came from a large family, she thought it would be best for him to live and work outside the home. But now he was all alone in Alaska. He asked me to go out with him—and I really wanted to—but I knew my parents would refuse.

I knew, however, that if my mother would listen to me, she would see the situation was unique. So I wrote a letter. She did understand, and I was allowed to date this young man until we were transferred again.

After thinking about these letters, I regretted that we hadn't continued the custom as I grew older. How nice it would have been to have letters that told me what my mother thought about life in general, that offered advice on what she thought was important, that cautioned me about the dangers of the world, that witnessed to her faith. I might not have wanted her to tell me those things in person. I probably would have thought she was interfering, but secretly I would have loved to have the letters—especially now that she is gone.

Thinking about that, I wrote the following letter to my children.

My Children,

There's so much I desire for each of you.

I want you to receive the education or training that will enable you to accomplish what you believe God wants you to do.

I want you to appreciate the beauty of God's world from the wide expanse of the seashore to the tiny wildflowers in your backyard.

I want you to value one another and the special bond that you share as members of this family and of God's family.

I want you and your spouse and children to recognize the importance of family—your individual family and your extended family.

I want you always to remember that you are loved—by me and by God.

I want you to identify the creative gifts God has given to you. The written word is my life's work, but I pray that you discover your medium: painting, crafts, photography, sewing, decorating, cooking, music, dance—whatever brings life and joy to your world.

I want you to know and enjoy your children. It seems like only yesterday that you were babies. I turned my back for a moment and you were grown.

I want you to treasure life. Take time each day for God and for yourself.

I want you never to be afraid to ask for help if you need it—and I want you to help each other. Ask God daily to help you love each other without judging, asking questions, or blaming.

I pray that God will lead you to fulfill the purpose He has designed especially for you.

Most important, I want you to "love the Lord your God with all your heart and with all your soul and with all your strength." I pray that my life has been a witness to you of the importance of faith and trust in God. If you believe in Father, Son, and Holy Spirit, I have kept my promise to God to raise you as His children too.

I pray that each of you has happiness, love, and wisdom in abundance, but most of all I pray that you have faith in Jesus as your Savior, who came to earth to live the perfect life you couldn't, to die, and to rise again to win for you forgiveness of sins and eternal life. You can trust His perfect love for you.

I love you,
Mama

I didn't exactly know when to give this letter to my children, so I decided to include it in this book, dedicated to all children from all mothers everywhere.

Slip a bookmark in at the right page, and give your daughter a copy. Will she think it's too sentimental? Possibly. Mushy? Probably. But maybe she'll forgive me. And perhaps she'll decide to pass it on to her own children some day.

Heavenly Father, help me to witness to my children and to other family members the love that I have for You. Thank You for Your letter to me—Your Holy Word. Let me find joy and strength in its pages every day. Use it to focus me on Your gracious actions on my behalf. In Jesus' name. Amen.

L.T.

I Quit!

In all these things we are more than con-
querors through Him who loved us.
Romans 8:37

"Four times seven is what?" I asked Jennifer as we studied fourth-grade math.

She wiggled in her chair, tapped her pencil on the
table, and searched the ceiling for the answer. "Um-mmmm,
24?" she offered.

"No, that's four times six," I corrected. "Try again."

After thinking for a while, Jennifer gave up in desperation. "I don't know. I'll never learn this stuff."

"Sure you will," I reassured her. "You just need to keep
going over it."

But my daughter wasn't convinced that she'd ever
remember the multiplication tables. Because I sensed her
frustration, I suggested we stop and try again later.

As the school year progressed, I noticed other school-
related fears looming on the horizon. Jennifer worried about
what would happen each day in the classroom. Everyday
tasks became gigantic, and I soon found that my once cheer-
ful and confident daughter was becoming unhappy and
apprehensive.

Jennifer came home from school one day and flung her
book bag on the floor. Collapsing on the couch in tears, she
announced, "I'm quitting the fourth grade!"

I stopped preparing supper and went to her. "Quitting,

huh? That's pretty serious. What happened?" I asked.

"It's too hard," she sobbed. "I have to know my times tables by heart, and there's too much work. The teacher expects us to do all this stuff by ourselves. I don't understand it and I never will."

I took my daughter in my arms and let her cry. Fourth grade was scary, all right. The children were expected to work independently, know multiplication and division, and handle a greater amount of homework and outside projects. And though Jennifer was a good student, these tasks seemed larger than life.

Sometimes we face battles that appear monstrous. Certainly the Israelites understood this when they faced the giant Goliath. This enormous Philistine champion stood more than 9 feet tall. He wore full armor, a helmet, and carried a javelin. From the Philistine lines, this imposing foe shouted his defiance against Israel. Can you imagine how intimidating he must have looked? (Probably just as frightening as a multiplication table to a fourth-grader!) The Israelites were terrified. How would they ever conquer this huge problem?

As you know, it was a simple shepherd boy who killed Goliath. David was prepared to fight this battle for two reasons. As an experienced shepherd, he had fought off lions and bears. He was strong and used to a good fight. More important, David wasn't afraid because he knew that the battle was the Lord's. David knew he wouldn't be fighting Goliath alone. He stood his ground and came against his enemy in the name of the God of the armies of Israel.

So it is in our life when we face enormous giants. Our loving and faithful God already has prepared us to fight the obstacles we'll meet. He has clothed us with the righteousness won for us by Christ on the cross. And He goes with us, for we are more than conquerors in His mighty name.

In time, Jennifer found that she could win the battle of numbers. With determination, she studied daily and eventually hit her target. (Puns intended!) She felled the mighty multiplication giant and moved boldly into the battle of division. Soon she'll tackle algebra, geometry, and maybe even trigonometry and calculus. And as my daughter wrestles with life's problems, I will continue to be by her side—shouting words of encouragement all the way! And God will be with her too, reminding her that she has the ultimate victory in Him.

> *Mighty God, be ever present with us as we fight the Goliaths in our lives. Thank You for the ultimate victory over sin, death, and the devil won for us by Jesus. In our Savior's name. Amen.*

N.O.B.

A Visit from the Grandchildren

Praise the LORD, O my soul; all my inmost being, praise His holy name. Praise the LORD, O my soul, and forget not all His benefits—who forgives all your sins and heals all your diseases, who redeems your life from the pit and crowns you with love and compassion, who satisfies your desires with good things so that your youth is renewed like the eagle's. Psalm 103:1–5

I don't think I worried too much about cuts and scrapes or bumps and falls when my children were young, but I seem to be determined to make up for it with my grandchildren.

From birth to about age 7, I worry about my grandchildren falling down the steps between our dining area and the bottom level of our home. Their parents seem perfectly comfortable when their babies crawl toward—or up and down—the stairs. They continue their conversations without a lapse when their toddlers stagger toward the stairway. They ignore the older youngsters when they leap from the top step, attempting to clear all three in a single swoop and land safely on the concrete floor below. I hold my breath, close my eyes, and grit my teeth.

The various modes of transportation at our houses cause a similar case of grandmotherly jitters. I try not to appear overly concerned about the bicycles, go-carts, minibikes, mountain bikes, and cars.

And I try to keep my thoughts about staying out past midnight to myself. But what's a grandmother to do?

I learned what a grandmother should *not* do when I invited all the grandchildren to spend the weekend with me. I planned several fun, safe methods of entertainment. It was close to Christmas, so we were going to bake Christmas cookies, watch nonviolent videos, make presents for their parents, and take a walk through the snowy woods.

My grandchildren ran through the videos, the cookies, and the presents in the first two hours. It took another 45 minutes to take our walk, and I still had more than 45 hours to go. We visited Hardees, the local video store, McDonalds, K Mart, Burger King, the local skating rink, and Pizza Palace at least twice from Friday afternoon to Sunday morning.

Because the weekend was so busy, I didn't have time to worry. Maybe that's why parents are less nervous than grandparents. Members of the older generation have more time to think about what could happen. Parents are too busy taking care of what is happening to worry about the "what ifs."

My grandmother was sometimes sharp-tongued, but I knew she loved us grandchildren. When we spent the week at her house, we snuggled into soft featherbeds, pulled the quilts up over our heads, and played "tents." We built play-houses in the woods and sawed holes through the roof of the woodshed to make secret doors. We rummaged through the barn and tried out the old Victrola. She also took us with her to buy groceries every Thursday and gave us money to buy a special dish from the hardware store for our playhouse.

When I think about it, there isn't much difference

between my outings with the grandkids and hers. Instead of the hardware store, we go to K Mart. Instead of playhouses, we play video games. And instead of sawing holes in the roof of the woodshed, my grandchildren prefer to see who can jump the farthest from the top step of the dining room stairs. But there's nothing more rewarding than a grandchild's hug and the touch of soft hands in yours. They can make you feel like a king or queen, as wise as Solomon, and as young as the wind.

I do think, however, that next time, I'll invite my grandchildren to visit one by one—that way I can spend quality time with each one.

> *Father, thank You for children and grandchildren who make life more fun. Thank You for Your great love for Your children—a love so incomprehensible that You sent Your only Son to suffer and die for our salvation. Help me live each day celebrating that I am Your chosen and loved child. In Jesus' name. Amen.*

L.T.

The Swimming Lesson

When you pass through the waters, I will
be with you; and when you pass through
the rivers, they will not sweep over you.
Isaiah 43:2

It was a beautiful Florida morning. The sky was a brilliant blue with only a few puffy white clouds dotting its glory. Jennifer and I were on our way to her first swimming lesson at a nearby pool. She was excited about being in the water on such a hot day. I was looking forward to watching my preschooler in action.

In the car she asked, "Mommy, will you watch me the whole time?"

"Of course I will. And afterward, when you're finished with your lesson, I'll get in the water and swim with you," I answered.

She giggled at the prospect that we'd be playing in the water together.

When we arrived, I slathered suntan lotion on my daughter and told her to have a good time. After meeting the swim instructor, I found a lounge chair under a palm tree, donned my straw hat, and sat back to watch my little one.

Jennifer took to the water like a duckling. She got her face wet, blew bubbles in the crystal-clear water, and kicked her legs while holding onto the edge of the pool. I enjoyed my part as "proud mommy" while I diligently watched my daughter's every accomplishment.

When the lesson was over, I slipped into the water and took Jennifer into my arms. Brushing a strand of wet hair from her eyes, I told her what a good job she'd done. Because she was doing so well and seemed so comfortable in the water, I suggested she try the next day's lesson—floating on her back.

"Mommy will be right here the whole time, Jennifer," I reassured her. "I won't let go of you. Relax and lie back in the water."

With one hand under her back and the other hand at her head, I moved her to a floating position. She seemed all right, but then I felt her body go rigid with fear. I pressed my hand up against her back so she could feel my presence and said, "It's okay. Mommy's right here."

"Noooo," she whined. "I'm scared. It's too deep."

"I won't let you sink. Calm down."

Suddenly, Jennifer began thrashing her arms. Her eyes filled with terror, and she began to cry.

"It's okay," I said as I grabbed her. Legs wrapped around me, she clung to me while I patted her back and whispered words of comfort. Holding her in my arms, I wondered why she didn't trust me. Why was she afraid when I was right there?

Then I understood. I remembered times when I had waded into something new. Fully submerged, I'd suddenly become paralyzed with fear when I focused on the deep waters of life that surrounded me. Although I knew that the Lord was holding me, I was reluctant to fully trust Him.

Over the years, I have discovered that God has held me up in all kinds of situations. Just as He planned for and secured my salvation, He is able to keep me safe. No matter where I go or what I do, I am in His keeping and He will never let me drown.

Heavenly Father, sometimes I feel like a scared little child. Hold me tightly so I may relax in the knowledge that You will keep my head above the deep waters of life. Thank You for saving me when I was drowning in my sins. In my Savior's name. Amen.

N.O.B.

Give and It Will Be Given

Give, and it will be given to you. A good
measure, pressed down, shaken together
and running over, will be poured into
your lap. For with the measure you use,
it will be measured to you. Luke 6:38

It was a Sunday afternoon, a week before Andy's wedding, and everyone's nerves were on edge.

Katie was going through some difficult times at
school—papers to write, chapters to read and outline, and
projects to complete for her work-study job, all by the same
quickly approaching deadline. She had arrived home on
Friday, and we went that night to pick up her bridesmaid's
dress from the dressmaker. Saturday morning, she got sick
and couldn't attend the bridesmaids' luncheon or finish her
homework. Now it was Sunday, and she had to return to
school in a few hours.

Mary was spending Sunday afternoon trying to gather
wedding clothes for her family. Her husband, Gary, and 13-
year-old son, Matthew, were groomsmen, 11-year-old Lydia
was a junior bridesmaid, and 4-year-old Marcus was the
ringbearer. Finding shoes and suitable outfits for the younger
children became a rather expensive venture for her part-
time salary. As if this weren't enough, Mary was the only
one of my daughters living nearby, so she was helping me
cook for the rehearsal dinner. Mary also was assisting the
bride's family with decorating and planning refreshments for
the reception.

Robin and her family, also caught up in the wedding preparations, had arrived for Sunday lunch. Her two boys, Luke and Sam, and her husband, Joe, also were groomsmen, and her daughter, Jenny, was the flower girl. Robin had spent Friday struggling to rearrange her work schedule. Unfortunately, she had been scheduled to be on call at the hospital the same weekend as the wedding. Her longtime coworker had left to accept another job and a new employee had been hired, which further complicated things. Robin had spent Saturday night shopping for Jenny's dress.

Somehow, someone managed to knock a glass of milk off the nightstand beside Katie's bed. It spilled directly into Katie's portable stereo/CD player. Robin, thinking that it was a glass Katie had left there, pointed it out to Katie. Mary cringed because she realized that Matthew had left it there Friday night when he had sat on Katie's bed—which, of course, Katie would rather he not do. Katie screamed. I tried to explain that it was my fault because I had suggested that Matthew and I watch TV in her room and I had meant to take the glass to the kitchen when the show was over. It didn't help that Robin can giggle at the most inappropriate times, and this happened to be one of them.

Robin started laughing as I ran for a towel to clean up the mess. Katie was ready to cry. And Mary tried to act like nothing was wrong as she pushed Matthew out of the room.

The next 30 minutes were rather strained. An hour later, however, Robin was helping Mary fill out her application for a full-time job at the post office where she currently worked part time. Katie was working on her paper. Matthew had fled the premises, and I was thanking God for sisters who forgive and forget.

I thought about the many ways my daughters give and take in their relationships with one another.

- As teenagers, Mary had locked Robin out of the house more than once. I learned later that they also had teamed up to replace a window in the storm door when it broke after being slammed shut.

- Mary "borrows" Katie's clothes when she's gone, and Katie marches down to her house to retrieve them. She also curls up on Mary's sofa to discuss boy problems.

- When Katie was born, Robin and Mary rejoiced. She was "their" baby as well as mine. When Robin was lying in the hospital in a coma, her sisters and brother rushed back from the beach to stay by her side, even sleeping on the floor of the waiting room, refusing to leave until she recovered.

- When Mary needs someone to stay with her children when she leaves for work at 4 A.M., Katie spends the night on her couch.

- And when Andy is married next Sunday, I'm confident all three girls will stand proudly beside him and welcome his new wife as another sister.

My girls have learned that being a sister means being willing to give to one another forgiveness, time, laughter, and love and being willing to give up anger, jealousy, and hurt feelings. It sounds like a sister's love is a lot like God's love.

Father, keep me from dwelling on that which hurts me and give me grace to forgive and forget. Remind me of Your grace-full gift of faith in my Savior, who has saved me from the evil thoughts and actions that would pull me under. Send Your peace to fill my heart and my family even in the midst of confusion. In Jesus' name. Amen.

L.T.

The Three-Legged Race

Let us run with perseverance the race
marked out for us. Let us fix our eyes on
Jesus, ... so that you will not grow
weary and lose heart. Hebrews 12:1–3

It was field day at Apollo Elementary. Everyone expected Jennifer and her friend Christy to win the three-legged race in their age group. Winning every practice run that their class held, the girls set their sights on a blue ribbon. However, they didn't consider the fact that they would have to race against all the classes in their grade.

As the coach tied a strip of soft fabric around the girls' legs, Jennifer's eyes searched for me in the crowd. I waved to her and yelled, "Go for it!" I gave her the thumbs-up sign. Smiling, she turned forward to concentrate on the race.

The whistle blew, and the race began. Jennifer and Christy started off quickly. Seconds later, they fell. As they scrambled to get up, I heard their classmates screaming, "Hurry, or you're gonna lose."

Beads of sweat formed across Jennifer's brow. Up and hobbling once again, the girls were no longer in first place. They strained against each other and often fell. When they finally reached the finish line, Jennifer's eyes were wet with tears, and her lower lip quivered. Instead of a blue ribbon, she sported red knees, muddy hands, and a badge of humiliation.

A tear trickled down my daughter's dirty face as I took

her aside. Burrowed in my arms, she whimpered, "It's all Christy's fault."

I wiped Jennifer's face with a tissue. "I'm sorry you both lost," I told her. "I love you, and I'm proud of you for finishing." After she had calmed down, I asked Jennifer if she had tried her best. She nodded her head.

"I think Christy tried her best too, don't you?" I asked.

Pushing the dirt with the toe of her sneaker, she didn't look at me. "Yeah, probably," came a whispered answer. Although my words didn't take away the sting of defeat, she learned a lesson in perseverance and good sportsmanship. Jennifer also learned that neither she nor Christy were infallible.

Failure and loss are part of life. But no matter how often Jennifer may fail, I want her to be able to learn from her mistakes, to move on, and not to worry about future failures.

I also want her to trust God and to believe that her heavenly Father is faithful to see her through a failure. He saw Adam and Eve through the first sin and promised them a Savior. He saw Naomi and Ruth through their hunger and made Ruth one of Jesus' ancestors. He saw David through his sin with Bathsheba and raised up the greatest King— Christ—from his line. Jesus saw Peter deny Him, yet He went to the cross to win forgiveness for this sin and all our sins. Then after His resurrection, Jesus urged Peter to feed His sheep and lambs.

We can hold on to God's promise that though a person may stumble, "he will not fall, for the LORD upholds him with His hand" (Psalm 37:24).

Over the years I've made a lot of mistakes—some even more than once. I've learned that though failure sometimes accompanies the challenges we face, God enables us to learn from our mistakes and to try again.

How to face failure is something I can teach my daughter. As she grows, she may do poorly on tests, feel let down if her team loses, or forget her lines in the school play. But when I show her how to use failure as a tool rather than as a stumbling block, she can ask God to help her learn from her mistakes and move on to success.

Dear God, instill in me the desire to persevere through all life's trials. Remind me that with You by my side, nothing is impossible. Amen.

N.O.B.

I Wish You Well

Suppose a brother or sister is without clothes and daily food. If one of you says to him, "Go, I wish you well; keep warm and well fed," but does nothing about his physical needs, what good is it?
James 2:15–16

Robin, Katie, Mary, and I were in New York for the first time in several years. We shopped, ate in great restaurants, and saw as many Broadway shows as time and money would allow.

The girls had traveled with me to New York on business trips in the past, so they knew the rules. Wear a shoulder bag and keep it close to your body. Don't ride the subway. Ignore the vendors and ticket sellers in the ticket line. Never look a homeless person in the eye. And never give anyone money. In fact, I had learned these rules so well that I carried my purses New York-style at home.

I had grown so accustomed to stepping around the homeless people that I did it as though no one were there. Mary couldn't do this. I could see the hurt in her eyes each time. "But, Mama," she had said on her first trip to the city, "what if he really does need food? And maybe her baby really is sick …"

She was only a teenager then, deserving of an answer, but I didn't want to examine my motives for saying no. On subsequent trips, I noticed Mary often turned back to look at those I passed by. "You can't do that," I said. "It only encourages them to beg. Besides, he would probably use whatever money you gave him to buy wine instead of food."

No matter how many times I had cautioned Mary, she acted the same on this trip. Several times I noticed her dropping behind to slip a homeless person a dollar or two or to hand them the hot coffee and breakfast roll she had bought but not tasted. She even had Robin and Katie rummaging through their pockets for change when they thought I wasn't looking.

I knew how hard it had been for my daughters to find the money for the trip. Mary and her husband have five children. Robin worked overtime to make the extra money, and Katie was a college student whose only income was from her work-study job. The money hadn't come easily for any of them.

Finally, I confronted them. "You're all letting the homeless people take advantage of you," I said. "They don't deserve your hard-earned money. You know the rules!"

Tears filled Mary's eyes as she looked at me. "I don't understand. Who made those rules? Doesn't God love them too?"

Suddenly, instead of grown-up daughters sitting on a hotel bed in the middle of Manhattan, I saw the little girls they had been—sitting attentively in their Sunday school class, in the church pew, around our kitchen table as we read about God and His great love for everyone. Of course God loves the people along the streets of New York City! What had I been thinking? If Jesus had been on the streets that day, He would have been the first to reach out to the "undeserving." After all, He gave His life on the cross to win forgiveness for all of us ("street" people, "country" people, "city" people, and "suburb" people), undeserving though we were.

I was ashamed of myself and my actions, but I was proud of the young women in front of me, proud they were my daughters. And I knew without a doubt that Jesus had been on the streets of New York City that morning. He had simply worked through the hearts and hands of three compassionate young women who remembered the lessons of their youth.

God, show me how to step out in love, even when it means taking a risk. Remind me that what I do for the least of these, I do for You. In Jesus' name. Amen.

L.T.

"No, I Won't!"

"For I know the plans I have for you,"
declares the LORD, "plans to prosper you
and not to harm you, plans to give you
hope and a future." Jeremiah 29:11

The very thought of the words "the terrible twos" usually sends chills down any mother's spine. Although we know that this necessary stage of development will lead to independence and growth, it can be a trying time for parent and child.

Having already experienced the twos with Matthew, I felt fairly secure in getting through this difficult time with Jennifer. Knowing that a 2-year-old's favorite word can be *no*, I tried to phrase my questions so she couldn't answer that way. For example, I knew better than to ask if she wanted a peanut butter and jelly sandwich for lunch. Instead, I asked, "Do you want a grilled cheese or a peanut butter and jelly sandwich?" That way she got a choice without an opportunity to tell me no.

This method also worked for many other toddler activities. When it was time to get dressed, I selected two different outfits and let Jennifer choose what to wear. This prohibited her from selecting colors and patterns that didn't match or putting on shorts and a T-shirt in the middle of winter.

One day, however, my easygoing toddler decided that Mommy's tried-and-true method was a part of the past.

With her spirit of independence at full blast, she was determined to have her way.

That morning she returned to her bedroom after breakfast. After a few minutes of complete silence, I became nervous that she was getting into trouble. I walked into her room and saw that she had gotten herself dressed. What a sight! She had put on her red and green flowered Christmas dress over her pink sweatpants, which had been turned inside out. Purple socks and yellow Big Bird slippers adorned her feet. To top it all off, she wore a "pretend" wedding veil my mother had made for her.

With less than an hour before a doctor's appointment, I wasn't very happy with her choice of clothing. If I brought her out with me in the 90-degree Florida heat, someone probably would take her away from me. I did what any other mother in this situation would do: I told her that she would have to change into something more appropriate for summer weather and for going out in public.

"No!" was her explicit answer. "I like this."

"But, sweetheart," I countered, "we have to go out, and it's too hot to wear all those clothes. Let's pick out something else."

"No, I don't wanna," was her firm answer.

Knowing that I had to think quickly, I pulled out two outfits for her to choose from. It didn't work. The battle continued. I offered to let her wear the Christmas dress if she took off the sweatpants, but she rejected that idea and some others as well.

This scenario made me wonder how my heavenly Father feels when I behave like a stubborn 2-year-old. There have been times when God has patiently given me a list of opportunities to serve Him and I've refused because I wanted to do things my way.

I am thankful that God doesn't give in to my selfish, nearsighted whims. Just as I wouldn't give up in seeking the best for my child, I know that my heavenly Father will continue to provide and care for me even when I don't cooperate. He even sent Jesus to earth to save uncooperative people like me.

How wonderful that He turns my *nos* into *yeses* and my tantrums into triumphs!

Father, thank You for Your love and patience. Thank You for sending Your Holy Spirit to change my uncooperative heart into one dedicated to serving You. Keep me open to the possibilities You present to me. In Jesus' name. Amen.

N.O.B.

Feelings or Faith?

Now faith is being sure of what we hope
for and certain of what we do not see.
Hebrews 11:1

I felt so alone as I walked into the intensive care unit.
My husband and the other children had gone home for
some much-needed rest. I always had felt so close to God,
and now when I really needed Him, it seemed like He was
nowhere to be found. Robin had been in an accident, and
she lay in a deep coma—one from which the doctors said
she might not wake up.

I overheard a technician and nurse discussing Robin's
condition when I walked into her room. "I'm afraid they're
going to have to face reality," the technician said. "She
probably will not live; and even if she does, she won't be
normal."

"That's right," the nurse agreed. "There's really no
hope—"

"I'm sorry, but you're wrong!" I interrupted. Suddenly it
didn't matter that my mind had been registering these same
thoughts, wondering if God had deserted us. In my heart, I
knew that God was on our side, and there was always hope.

"Robin may be in a coma," I said, "but Jesus is alive. As
long as He is alive, there is always hope!"

What had I been thinking anyway—that God had
taken a walk around the block and was letting us go through
this alone? No, He had sent Jesus into this world to walk

with us, to go to the cross for our salvation, to rise again to give us the promise of eternal life. Jesus promised that He would never leave us. And He had been with us the whole time: in the words of my Bible, which I had grabbed as we rushed to the car; in the arms of our pastor, who met us at the hospital and prayed with us; and in the phone calls and prayerful support of friends and relatives.

I found out that afternoon that our feelings aren't a true indicator of God's presence. Sometimes we have to stand on what we know is true, even when we feel otherwise.

More strong feelings—and even stronger cries of praise and thanksgiving to God—surfaced later that week when Robin opened her eyes and spoke to us.

Thank You, Father, for being there when I need You … even when I don't recognize You. Amen.

L.T.

Tuned Out

Call to Me and I will answer you and
tell you great and unsearchable things
you do not know. Jeremiah 33:3

I'm thankful that my daughter likes to talk. I don't mean an incessant rambling that can drive you crazy. I mean the heart-to-heart talk that lets me in on her life and binds us closer together.

I've found that as my daughter has grown, our conversations have changed—not just in content, of course, but in the way in which she wants me to respond.

The changes began when she entered adolescence. Up to that point, she willingly listened when I offered suggestions or advice. When Jennifer entered sixth grade though, everything changed.

One day Jennifer was discussing her favorite subject—boys—when she stopped talking right in the middle of a sentence.

"Jennifer?" I asked.

"What?"

"You didn't finish your sentence. What were you going to say?" I prompted.

"Never mind," came her terse answer.

"Why won't you tell me?" I prodded.

"Because." Silence filled the room. "Because I know what you will say."

My preteen had applied the brakes on her discourse and

tuned me out before I had an opportunity to speak. Trying to jump start our conversation, I gave her my opinion on the subject we had been discussing.

Since that wasn't what she wanted to hear, her posture stiffened and her lips sealed. As far as she was concerned, the conversation was over.

After a quick prayer, however, I was ready to handle her attitude. I asked Jennifer to sit down so we could talk. I explained that I wanted us to be open with each other and that it was okay for me to express my opinions and to give advice. After all, that's part of my job as a mother.

After we talked for a while, Jennifer realized that because I had been through similar situations, I probably knew a good way to handle things. She also realized that I wanted to help her because I love her.

Reflecting on my life, I discovered that I'm guilty of doing exactly what my daughter did. Sometimes I tune out God because I know what He'll say. I stubbornly refuse to talk to the very Person who has all the answers. I don't want to hear as He points out my sins or offers the reassurance of forgiveness for Jesus' sake. But God sends His Holy Spirit to break down my defenses and restore our relationship.

As my daughter has matured, she has come to realize that I only have her best interests at heart. Now that she understands that I can be trusted with her secrets, dreams, and problems, she comes to me often and our bond has grown even stronger.

The Holy Spirit has strengthened my trust in my heavenly Father to see me through the challenges of life. Knowing that God's ears are open to my every cry (Psalm 34:15) has enabled me to pour out my heart to Him without fear or reservation. Our relationship has become stronger as I focus on His desires for me.

> *Heavenly Father, help me to be a good listener and to keep an open mind so my daughter always will feel comfortable talking with me. Refresh me daily as I read Your Word and talk with You in prayer. Motivate me by Your Spirit to seek Your will and remain open to Your leading. In Jesus' name. Amen.*

N.O.B.

To My Daughter-in-law on Your Wedding Day

But the greatest of these is love.
1 Corinthians 13:13b

Paul spoke of love when he wrote: "If I speak in the tongues of men and of angels, but have not love, I am only a resounding gong or a clanging cymbal" (1 Corinthians 13:1).

To love means to cherish. I know that you are aware the love the two of you share is rare today, but perhaps you don't know how difficult it will be to maintain. Together, nourish your love with faith and loyalty. Help it to grow by speaking its language honestly and openly and never being ashamed of the excitement you find in each other.

Paul spoke of lasting love when he wrote: "If I have the gift of prophecy and can fathom all mysteries and all knowledge, and if I have a faith that can move mountains, but have not love, I am nothing" (1 Corinthians 13:2).

To love means to devote yourself to another, to put your loved one's happiness before your own. That is impossible to do on your own, but when you love with the love of God, it becomes easy. Agree together to love each other with a devotion that ties you together in God and allows you to reach out and include others in that love.

Paul spoke of true love when he wrote: "Love is patient, love is kind. It does not envy, it does not boast, it is not proud. It is not rude, it is not self-seeking, it is not easily angered, it keeps no record of wrongs" (1 Corinthians 13:4–5).

To love means to give someone a second chance and a third and a fourth and a ... A love as true as yours learns to forget as well as to forgive, to always see the best in the other, to pledge never to be angry at the same time, and to love with an everlasting love. You have the privilege of offering forgiveness because you both have been forgiven by your heavenly Father for Jesus' sake.

Paul spoke of a trusting love when he wrote: "Love does not delight in evil but rejoices with the truth. It always protects, always trusts, always hopes, always perseveres" (1 Corinthians 13:6–7).

To love means to trust when times get rough, to rejoice in the good times and have faith in the bad, to protect when the other needs a defender, to cling to God and each other when hope seems far away.

Paul spoke of never-ending love when he wrote: "Love never fails.... These three remain: faith, hope and love. But the greatest of these is love" (1 Corinthians 13:8, 13).

To love means to strengthen each other with faith, to lift each other with hope, to cherish each other with the greatest gift one can give another: true love.

Lord, thank You for showing me what love is in the person of Jesus Christ. Thank You for His love that even death could not contain. With Him alive in me, help me to love another selflessly and faithfully. In my Savior's name. Amen.

L.T.

Not My Daughter!

He who dwells in the shelter of the Most High will rest in the shadow of the Almighty. I will say of the LORD, "He is my refuge and my fortress, my God, in whom I trust." Psalm 91:1–2

I stood in my bedroom folding laundry when I heard the front door slam. Jennifer came to the doorway and asked, "Mom, can I go to Rhonda's* house to play?"

"Sure," I answered, barely looking up from my work.

Quiet invaded the room for a moment, then Jennifer said, "Becky's* mom won't let her go there anymore."

Her comment intrigued me. "Why is that?" I asked.

"Because Rhonda's daddy touched her where he isn't supposed to," Jennifer answered.

Feeling light-headed, I grabbed for the bedpost. All I could think of was, *That poor little girl.* As the magnitude of this discovery hit me, my next thought was, *Oh, God, no! Did he touch my daughter?* If he had, would she tell me? I knew that pedophiles threaten their victims to keep their actions secret.

I sat on the bed and motioned for Jennifer to sit next to me. Once we were eye-to-eye, I asked, "Did Rhonda's daddy ever touch you?"

"No."

"Are you sure, Jennifer? If he's touched you and told you not to tell anyone, that's wrong. That would be a bad secret to keep," I said.

*name has been changed

"Mommy, I promise. He never did. Now, can I go and play with Rhonda?" she asked.

I couldn't believe her question. I wanted to scream, "No! Of course you can't go! It's not safe." But I didn't. Jennifer enjoyed playing with her friend. She hadn't been hurt, and as a 7-year-old, she didn't fully understand the situation.

What do I say, Lord? I asked. *Help me to deal with this.*

I gulped back my fear and anger. "Jennifer, I want to talk to Rhonda's mother first," I finally said. "Why don't you call Rhonda and ask her to come over here today."

That day will stay in my memory forever. For a while, I was overprotective. I allowed fear to grab me by the throat and squeeze until trust was almost gone. I felt like a mother lioness ready to pounce on anything that might harm my innocent offspring.

As mothers, we are faced with the realities of this world. Sometimes they're ugly and we need the protection, strength, and wisdom that can come only from our heavenly Father. When I asked God for help and direction, I knew how to deal with this problem. My peace was restored, Jennifer was protected, and she continued to see Rhonda under supervised conditions.

If you're afraid, turn to God. He has walked through the valley of the shadow of death so you might have forgiveness and eternal life. He also will walk with you through any problem that may be facing you or your daughter.

O God, remind me that I don't need to be afraid because You are always with me. Amen.

N.O.B.

I Was Wrong, I'm Sorry

*Therefore confess your sins to each other
and pray for each other so that you may
be healed. James 5:16*

I remember telling Katie about Catherine Marshall, a
great writer and woman of faith. "She wrote for *Guideposts*,"
I told her. "She also wrote wonderful inspirational books
about Christian living and prayer. That's what I'd like to
do—be the next Catherine Marshall."

At the time, I meant that I'd like my writing to follow
the pattern she laid down. I wasn't comparing my spiritual
life to hers. I did that later.

I did it the very next day, in fact, which was a bad day.
Someone backed into my car. When I went to the insurance
company, the office manager treated me rudely. "I don't
believe her attitude," I muttered self-righteously as I stormed
out of the office. "I'd never act like that!"

When I arrived home, I made a bad day worse by
yelling at Katie about a sweater she had borrowed and forgotten to return to my closet—the very same daughter I had
talked to so piously the day before.

I wasn't that angry about what she'd done, I was just
taking my frustration out on her. "But, Mama, I was going
to—" she tried to interrupt. I didn't give her the opportunity to explain. And while I was shouting at her, I could hear
God asking me, "My child, why do you return to that
behavior from which I have set you free?" But I clung stub-

bornly to my "rights" and continued to rant and rave.

Later as I reflected on the incident, I realized what a bad example I had set. I wanted to be the writer that Catherine Marshall was, but it might be better if I first tried to be the Christian woman she appeared to be. I had been wrong. I needed to apologize to Katie. And I needed to apologize to my heavenly Father. After I confessed my sin, I asked Him to help me offer my daughter a better example.

I spoke with Katie the next morning before she returned to college. "Honey, I'm sorry," I said. "I was wrong to talk to you in that way. I know you just forgot to return the sweater. Will you forgive me?"

"It's all right, Mama," she said. "We all have bad days. I was getting ready to put the sweater back in your closet. But I really should have done it sooner."

Katie left for school with a smile on her face, and I sat down to think about what had happened. My desire to live as a Christian had been put to the test—not just with Katie, but with the office manager at the insurance company. I had failed.

I didn't know what may have happened to the office manager to cause her to treat me so rudely. Even if she was rude on purpose, I could forgive her and ask for her forgiveness for my attitude as well. Although the woman hadn't asked for my forgiveness, that wasn't the point. We can never earn forgiveness for things we do. So Jesus came to earth to live the perfect life we couldn't, face the capital punishment that was rightfully ours, and rise again to assure us of God's forgiveness for all our sin. In the same way, we are called to extend the hand of forgiveness to others. "I forgive her, Lord," I told God, "just like You and Katie forgave me."

Some of the most difficult times in our Christian life occur when we try to relate to others—especially family members. We know how we are supposed to act, but we have a tendency to toss aside grace and mercy and hang on stubbornly to our grievances. Instead, we have the privilege to extend forgiveness to those who wrong us. Sometimes these uncomfortable, even embarrassing, situations are opportunities for the Holy Spirit to work in our lives to help us follow Christ's example.

Dear God, thank You for Your forgiveness for Jesus' sake. Help me to let go of the pain I feel when someone hurts me. Teach me to extend the same loving forgiveness to others that You have extended to me. In my Savior's name. Amen.

L.T.

Love Knots

~tie your love together with these ideas

Challenge Yourself

1. **Challenge your routine.** Plan to do something new as mother and daughter every few months. List activities that both of you always have wanted to do—going to the opera or ballet, learning how to fish or play a new board game, taking dance lessons, reading a particular book of the Bible, or reading a classic Christian book. Then execute your plan.

2. **Challenge modern technology.** Buy nice stationery and colorful pens and set aside one hour every two weeks as a letter-writing night—a time for your daughter and you to communicate with friends and distant relatives. Teach her to appreciate the beauty of a handwritten letter in this modern age of the cell phone, fax, and e-mail. Include favorite Bible verses or news from your church activities in these letters.

3. **Challenge your finances.** Open a joint checking account with your teenage daughter. Help her set up a budget and learn to use her money wisely. Discuss tithing and why we offer the

firstfruits of our labor to the Lord.

4. **Challenge your benevolence.** Find a local agency, organization, or church group that needs volunteers and work together as mother and daughter. Opportunities may include reading books to the blind, preparing meals, or doing yard work for older adults.

5. **Challenge your fears.** If you or your daughter worry a lot or become fearful in new situations, work together to choose Bible verses that express comfort and hope. Write these on index cards and keep them in a purse, book bag, locker, or desk drawer. Then when God's Word of encouragement is needed, pull out a card. You might include simple prayer starters for common situations, such as tests, storms, accidents, etc. As you work, talk about your fears and how you have seen God at work to overcome fear.

6. **Challenge family knowledge.** Challenge your daughter to learn more about her family heritage by tracing her family tree. Use the library, genealogy clubs, newsletters, and the Internet as resources. This would be a good time to discuss why family is important. Emphasize your inclusion in the family of God.

7. **Challenge self-concept.** To boost your daughter's self-esteem, compliment her once a day. Base your compliments on something more

than physical attractiveness, such as behavior, personality traits, attitude, schoolwork, household chores, or relationship skills. Remind your daughter often of her source of self-esteem— the value God places on her as His special daughter. Our heavenly Father loves *her* so much that He sent His only Son to save *her* from eternal death.

8. **Challenge anonymous giving.** Secretly do something for someone else at least once a month. Make and deliver May baskets, buy coloring books and crayons for a hospital children's ward, or mail a gift certificate to someone in need. Discuss the satisfaction it brings to give without recognition. As you discuss your projects and the reasons behind these actions, emphasize that we give to others in thanksgiving for all that Jesus has given to us.

9. **Challenge the negativity of the secular media.** Work as a mother-daughter reporting team to uncover good news. Make your own newsletter or mock newspaper. Write about important times in the lives of your family and friends. Illustrate the newspaper with photographs or drawings. Don't forget to include important spiritual milestones, such as baptisms, confirmations, Bible verses that were memorized, and the like.

10. **Challenge fear of speaking.** Since most people fear speaking in public, develop dramas with

your mother and/or daughter to perform as a family. You might even organize a drama group at your church or school. Encourage each other to read aloud. Take turns preparing and presenting family devotions. These simple options will strengthen your ability to speak in front of people and, more important, to witness your faith with confidence in God's guidance.

GROWTH

Prayer

Dearest Father,

Remind me daily that I can trust You as a child trusts her earthly parents. Let my daughter be my example of faith as I watch her grow from infant to child, child to teen, and teen to woman.

Show us both that growth is more than a physical or mental process. It is a spiritual one as well. Grant us an extra measure of Your Holy Spirit that we may grow in obedience to You and in humility, service, and love toward others. Rather than measuring each other by feet or inches, dress or shoe size, help us measure each other with Your eyes.

Sometimes I believe that I need to be strong, wise, and all-knowing. After all, I'm the parent. Remind me that I don't have all the answers. Only You do, and I have the privilege of being a child too—Your child.

Bless our physical and mental growth. May Your Word and Your Supper feed our spiritual growth as we grow from child to adult and adult to child. In Jesus' name. Amen.

What Would People Think?

How precious to me are Your thoughts,
O God! Psalm 139:17

I don't know where I got the impression that I was supposed to be perfect. Perhaps it was normal rebellion against
my mother, who, in my teenage years, I thought was far
from perfect. She embroidered yellow roses on pillowcases
for hours, fabric spread all over. The tables held stacks of
books, which she read one after the other. The dishes often
went unwashed while she spent time with my brother or me.

Embroidery was acceptable, if it was a pillowcase for my
bed. Messiness was fine, when I was younger, and reading
was great, if it was to me, but as I grew older these things
became a problem. I was embarrassed to let the Sunday
dishes sit in the sink while Mom played a game with my
brother or urged me to take a walk with her to find the first
wild strawberries of the spring. What would people think if
they saw our dirty house?

Throughout my school years, I wanted to improve my
grades. Not because my mother complained—she thought I
was perfect. I wanted to improve because I knew that I was-
n't perfect. When I made Bs, I was disappointed. I wanted
to make straight As. Once I thought I would die when I
received a D on a chemistry test. It didn't matter that when
the class ended, I had earned an A. All I could remember
was that D. What would people think?

Later, I wanted to have the perfect house, the perfect

children, and the perfect marriage. But my house was never problem free. My children were seldom angels, and my marriage was in trouble. I tried to keep up a front. I didn't want anyone to know we had problems. After all, what would people think?

So I went to church every Sunday, taught Sunday school, became church training director and youth director, and participated on every committee. I would even try to finish all my housework on Saturday so I didn't have to "work" on Sunday. If I couldn't be perfect, at least I could be a "good" Christian. I ran myself ragged chairing committee meetings and preparing Bible studies. If I turned down a request or said no, what would people think?

Then I saw my daughter acting the same way, and I realized how wrong I was. Robin was turning into a replica of me. Her children had to be dressed perfectly, and she had to be the efficient employee, the compassionate church member, the adoring wife, and the all-knowing mother—at all times. As I watched her interact with her daughter, I wondered if she was taking time to enjoy Jenny.

I remembered the day Robin was born, the little girl I'd always wanted. As I looked at her tiny fingers and wrinkled little face, I wondered what she'd be when she grew up, what kind of woman she'd become. I wanted her to be a success at whatever she undertook.

Now as I watched Robin with her own daughter, I suddenly recognized that my mother's relaxed style of living was worth trying after all. Here was the little girl I loved so much, all grown up, and I had never taken a walk with her just to look for wild strawberries. I had never embroidered a pillowcase for her, and I had read very few books to her.

"Robin," I said, interrupting as she tried to remove a stain from Jenny's dress. "Why don't you stick her dress in the washing machine? I think there's a pair of jeans here that one of the boys left that would probably fit her."

"But, Mama," Robin said, a grin spreading across her face, "it's Sunday. I thought we weren't supposed to wash clothes on Sunday. What would people think?"

My laughter joined hers. "In my old age, I'm beginning to realize that it's what God thinks that's important. I believe even He would agree that some rules are made to be broken—especially if they're silly, human-made rules of perfectionism."

I looked at the dishes from our Sunday meal still scattered on the table and turned and ruffled Jenny's short brown hair. The Bible says, "Pursue righteousness, godliness, faith, love, endurance and gentleness" (1 Timothy 6:11), but I don't remember a thing about spotless clothes or clean dishes or perfect grades. "When you get your jeans on, the three of us are going to take a walk," I told Jenny. "I know a place down in the pasture where wild strawberries used to grow."

Lord, help me to learn to measure excellence and success by who I am in Christ. Lead me in my walk as Your daughter and help me to measure myself by no one's standards but Yours. Remind me that growing spiritually is not about reaching some human concept of perfection. It's about living in the grace that is mine because of Christ's perfection. In His name. Amen.

L.T.

Where Have the Years Gone?

*My days are swifter than a runner; they
fly away. Job 9:25*

It was a cold, wet December morning. I had returned
home from taking Jennifer to grade school. The house was
quiet except for the sound of raindrops pelting the windows.
I put some water in the microwave for a cup of tea and wandered into Jennifer's room. *What a mess*, I thought as I
picked up her nightgown from the floor. After tripping over
a stuffed animal, I decided that my morning would be well
spent cleaning her bedroom.

With my cup of hot tea within easy reach, I began picking up. On my daughter's bed lay an outfit that she had
decided not to wear. She had said it was too small. *What
other clothes has she outgrown?* I wondered as I peered into
her closet.

Hanging among Jennifer's everyday clothes, I found a
Christmas dress that my mother had sewn many years ago.
Jennifer had worn the dress as an infant, but it had
remained in the closet as a reminder of her grandmother's
love and skill. I pulled out the dress and admired the expert
work my mother had done. As I traced my fingers across the
delicate lace collar, I had a hard time believing that my
daughter was once small enough to wear this dress.

I remembered what a good baby Jennifer had been. She
had such an easygoing disposition, usually happy and coo-
ing. Even better, she quickly slept through the night, mak-

ing her mother a happy person as well! Because she was born prematurely, Jennifer had been tiny. Not even five pounds at birth, she was too small for most of her clothes when we brought her home from the hospital. After several weeks, though, I was able to dress her in dainty dresses, pink stretch suits, and pastel sleepers. Building on my experiences with my son, I looked forward to fussing over a little girl.

As a toddler, my daughter was adventuresome and curious. She examined everything and always asked why. She enjoyed keeping up with her brother, even though he was six years older. The age difference never seemed to stop her from trying to be "one of the boys."

During preschool and her early elementary years, Jennifer blossomed. She was eager to learn, whether she was at school or at a dance lesson. She was a good student, a cooperative child, and a caring individual. God blessed us greatly with this precious little girl.

Before we knew it, Jennifer had braces on her teeth, her boyfriend's name plastered all over her books, and the telephone attached to her ear. *Where had the years gone?* I wondered.

My "little girl" was growing up before my eyes. Suddenly I felt old as I held my daughter's baby dress. There would be no more babies for me. Soon my preteen's emerging independence would mean that she wouldn't need me as much. It wouldn't be cool for her to walk with me around the mall or for us to go to movies together. She would be going on her first date, leaving for the prom, and preparing for high school graduation. Then there would a wedding and eventually pretty pink dresses bought for her daughter ...

Enough! My wandering mind snapped back to the present, and I put the baby dress back in Jennifer's closet. I couldn't handle that kind of time travel. Right now—today—Jennifer was still in elementary school. I was determined to keep her there for a little while longer.

I picked up my cup of tea, now cold, and headed back to the kitchen to reheat it. The rain slowed to a drizzle, and the sun peeked out from the gray clouds. Perhaps today wasn't such a good day to go through Jennifer's closet. Maybe it should wait until Saturday. Then Jennifer could take a stroll down memory lane with me—before time got away from us.

O Creator God, thank You for the precious gift of a daughter. May the ties of Your love bind our mother-daughter relationship and make it stronger. Help me imitate the love You have shown to me in Your Son, Jesus, whose sacrifice on the cross redeemed me. Help me appreciate each day I have with my loved ones. In His name. Amen.

N.O.B.

Planting Seeds

Still other seed fell on good soil. It came
up and yielded a crop, a hundred times
more than was sown. Luke 8:8

It was two weeks before Christmas. Robin, Mary, Katie, Andy's fiancée, Christy, and I decided to go shopping at an outlet center about three hours away. We left early on Saturday morning to spend the day together. Though there were a few minor disagreements, we got along well for 16 fun-filled hours.

We almost got lost in an early snowstorm, laughed until other customers stared at us, and renewed our relationships with one another. We remembered why we loved one another and why we still preferred to have our own rooms. The outing was a wonderful reunion for the sisters, the almost sister-in-law, and the mother. It was truly seed well sown. We came away with a renewed sense of family and already had made plans to do it again.

Not long ago, I realized that I needed to renew my relationship with the Bible. Through my time spent with the Word, God renews my spirit. I thought about the way the girls and I still laughed over the things that happened that Saturday. Our time together helped us not only to bear our differences but also to appreciate them. It gave us new perspective and reminded us of the love between us that we often take for granted.

Reading the Bible is like reading a letter from a loved

one. Each time we read God's Word, we are reminded of His great love for us. This love caused God to send Jesus, love incarnate, to be our Savior from sin. This love caused God to send His Holy Spirit to work faith in Jesus in our hearts. This love causes God to keep us firmly rooted in the faith. Because of God's love in Christ, we are free to love others.

God, send me Your Holy Spirit to encourage me to dedicate myself anew to reading Your Word. Help me appreciate the nourishment it brings to my life. Amen.

L.T.

When Will I Grow Up?

There is a time for everything, and a season for every activity under heaven.
Ecclesiastes 3:1

"This dress makes me look fat," Jennifer lamented as she plopped herself down on the chair in the fitting room. "Nothing looks good on me, Mom. When am I gonna grow up so I can be taller and thinner?"

I walked over to her and smoothed the silky brown hair from her face. Tears welled up in her eyes, her unhappiness with her current appearance all too apparent.

"I think you're beautiful, Jennifer," I told her as I cupped her chin in my hand.

"Yeah, right," she answered, avoiding my eyes.

"You are. God made you just right—for right now. Pretty soon you'll sprout up," I said. "But you know, there will be other things that might bother you."

Jennifer looked at me. "What do you mean?" she asked.

"Your body will change and develop in ways that will prepare you to be a woman. You'll have to deal with acne, shaving your legs, and monthly mood swings," I explained.

"Yuck," she answered, then fell quiet. "Maybe I should try on the jumper," she said after a pause.

I smiled and handed her the A-line, hides-the-lumps, classic dress. "Yes, dear, I think this one will look great on you."

Father God, help me appreciate and enjoy what makes me special today, rather than wishing for what I think will be better tomorrow. Always remind me of the value You gave to me in my Baptism when You made me Your precious daughter through the redeeming work of Jesus on the cross. In my Savior's name. Amen.

N.O.B.

A New Day's Growth

The earth is the LORD'S, and everything in it. Psalm 24:1a

Growing up in the country gave my children an appreciation for the wonderful creation God has given us. Katie loves the fields and trees that surround our farm and the narrow creek that runs through the woods. As a child, she and her brother, Andy, spent summer days climbing the trees and splashing in the cold, clear water, which spouts from several springs. Each winter, they would sled down steep banks. Springtime meant watching the bluebirds nest.

When Katie entered kindergarten, her teacher helped each child plant a maple seedling in a paper cup. The children brought the seedlings home to transplant into their own yards. I'm sure some of the kids spilled their plant or left the paper cup on the bus. But not Katie. She cradled her seedling in her hands until she got home.

"Mom!" she yelled as she walked into the house. "Guess what? I've got my very own tree!" She stationed the tiny tree on the sunny window sill above the kitchen sink and watered it until it was large enough to transplant. Then she and her dad planted it in a protected area beside our driveway.

Every day, Katie checked her tree. I was certain it wouldn't survive the cold North Carolina winters or the hot, dry summers. Instead, the tree thrived and grew up with Katie. Like her, it seemed to sprout overnight into a strong, sturdy specimen. It seemed only a moment until the tree towered overhead and Katie began college.

Environmental biology, one of her first classes at Gardner-Webb University, fascinated Katie and prompted her to plunge headlong into the study of environmental issues. One day, she accompanied me on a visit to one of my clients, who lives in the mountains. As we were returning, we saw a sign opposing dumping chemicals into the river. It alleged that a plant further up the mountain was at fault. Handmade posters protesting the protesters were staked near the sign.

"Mom, why don't Christians take their responsibility to the earth more seriously?" Katie asked. "Some Christians, even some of the students, think of environmental concerns as a joke. They make fun of people who want to recycle or keep the waters clean. Some of my classmates laughed at me the other day because I refused to let them throw Styrofoam cups out of my car window. Don't they realize how important the trees and the rivers and the streams are to us?"

Until that moment, I hadn't paid too much attention to the environment either. I hadn't consciously connected the natural world God created to my lifestyle. Of course, I was thankful for the tall trees that surrounded our home and the meadows that stretched peacefully alongside it, but I took it all for granted.

The next morning I went to my office as usual to sit quietly and read my Bible. The office is "my" place, a spot where I always can spend time with my Lord. It is a converted back porch with large windows that wrap comfortably around its shoulders. A huge maple tree drapes itself over the roof above my desk. The leaves from the giant limbs caress the eaves with their brilliant colors in the fall. Snow cuddles down into the hollow of the branches in the winter—the same branches that make a playground for squirrels in the summer. In the spring, the new leaves form a fresh frame for the sun as it rises over the distant mountains. I marvel at it all.

As I sat there that morning, I thought about what Katie had said. The maple tree was like a cathedral to me. Everything about it made me think of God, just as each element of the medieval cathedral was planned to teach illiterate worshipers about God.

This tree welcomed each day God gave with outstretched branches, yearning for the sun. In the same way, I start each day with God in His Word, yearning for His salvation message. The wood reminded me of the cross on which my Savior died, and the tiny buds of spring and the green leaves of summer brought to mind Christ's resurrection. God had put the plan for this tree within a tiny seed, just as He had planned for me before I was born and formed me in my mother's womb.

That morning, I asked God to help me better appreciate His gifts in nature and to become a better caretaker of His creation. Perhaps someday, my great-grandchild will look into the branches of Katie's tree and realize that our gracious God loved us enough to give us wonderful gifts such as tall trees, clear streams, and, most important, His Son.

Father, thank You for the earth and its fullness. Remind me of my privilege to preserve the natural beauty and resources You have provided. Allow me, as Your child, to appreciate more fully the wonder and order of the world You created. I praise You for Your gifts, especially for the gift of Your Son. In His name. Amen.

L.T.

Basic Training

Train a child in the way he should go,
and when he is old he will not turn from
it. Proverbs 22:6

"Watch this," Jennifer told her girlfriend. Holding a dog biscuit in her hand, my daughter called to our poodle.

"Suzy, here!" Jennifer pointed her index finger toward her feet. Obediently, a tiny bundle of curly black fur ran across the room and sat directly in front of her.

"Good girl," Jennifer cooed as she gave Suzy the treat. "Now lay down. Play dead. Good dog!" Jennifer beamed as her furry friend obediently complied.

When our family first talked about getting a puppy, my husband and I discussed the responsibilities of owning a dog. Of course, both our children promised they'd help with the chores. "We could even teach her tricks," Jennifer suggested.

"That would be fun," I said. "But she also must know the basics—like 'sit,' 'stay,' and 'here.' And we all need to be involved in the training because our dog needs to obey every one of us."

When Suzy was about five months old, I enrolled her in obedience training. Each Saturday morning, we learned the fundamentals. Sitting in lawn chairs on the sidelines, the kids watched as Suzy and I practiced with the other participants. My children heard the instructions from the teacher and watched the dogs and their owners respond to the command being taught. During the week, everyone practiced what Suzy and I had learned. In time, Suzy learned the basic commands as well as some neat tricks.

The experience gave me an insight about parenting. I need to be consistent and clear with my children. After all, how can I expect my daughter to grow into a godly woman if she doesn't understand what it means to live out her Christian faith? So we attend church and Sunday school as a family and encourage one another to read our Bibles on a regular basis. In addition to this immersion in His Word, I daily ask God to make me a positive role model for my children.

God says in Deuteronomy 4:9: "Be careful, and watch yourselves closely so that you do not forget the things your eyes have seen or let them slip from your heart as long as you live. Teach them to your children and to their children after them."

One of the things I teach Jennifer and Matthew is what God expects of His beloved children. But because we cannot obey God's commands, it is also my privilege as a parent to share the precious message of the Gospel and the forgiveness that is ours for Jesus' sake. My children know that we can't be perfect on our own, but that Jesus came to be our perfection.

Just as Suzy needed basic training to learn how to be an obedient pet, we all, children and adults, need unwavering instruction in the faith. As we study God's Word and partake of His precious body and blood, the Holy Spirit is at work in our lives to strengthen us and enable us to grow in Christ-likeness and obedience to His commands.

Dear Father, send Your Holy Spirit to work obedience in my heart, not to fulfill some obligation but to celebrate the freedom You have given me through faith in Jesus. Help me to teach Your ways to my daughter and to encourage her as she grows as Your child. In Jesus' name. Amen.

N.O.B.

There Is Honor— and Growth—in Work

Be strong and courageous, and do the work. Do not be afraid or discouraged, for the LORD God, my God, is with you.
1 Chronicles 28:20

The day started badly. In fact, the whole week had been rough. Two of my clients had books being released the next week. I was trying to arrange autograph parties, pick up books from the printer, and prepare advertising and promotion copy, but my computer was being stubborn. It worked sometimes, and sometimes it didn't. If this weren't enough, I still needed to finish three stories for *Guideposts*. I was discouraged, disheartened, and desperate.

Then my daughter Mary walked into my office and asked me to watch her 4-year-old, Marcus. Her employer had called unexpectedly and asked her to fill in for someone who was sick. As I looked at her imploring face, I recalled her excitement when she applied for the position with the postal service. The benefits package was attractive and the salary was good, but she had been scared too.

To apply for the job, Mary had to drive about 100 miles to Charlotte for a series of grueling tests. "It will mean driving through all that early morning commuter traffic," she had said. "And I don't know where I'm going, and they say the tests are terribly hard …"

Because I had known the importance of the job, I

offered to baby-sit Marcus while she interviewed. I also helped her select what to wear and loaned her our car. As I watched her prepare to leave for the tests, I knew she needed strength and reassurance that she could do the job. While I could give her encouragement, she really needed God's strength and courage.

I prayed for Mary as she left for the long drive to Charlotte. I prayed for her when she got the job and when her baby-sitter became ill and she had to scramble for an alternative because I was out of town. I prayed for her when four bundles of mail fell apart in the backseat of her car and again when it snowed.

Even everyday work-related problems can seem unbearable. Things can get worse and worse, all in one morning, until we want to throw up our hands and walk away. But God is strong when we are not!

As I stood with Marcus at the door waving good-bye to his mother, I knew that what I needed more than a new computer, a new job, or a coffee break, was a prayer break. Though determination is a vital ingredient when performing our work, our jobs demand more than our own determination can provide. We need God's assurance that we are following His path. When we ask for His help, whether it's for ourselves or for our daughter, God will renew our vitality and excitement. Like He did for Moses, He will provide someone to hold up our arms when we tire. Like He did for Jesus, He will provide respite. Like He did for Paul and Peter, He will provide guidance and direction.

And when we fail at our jobs, God is there to assure us of His love and to strengthen our faith in the work of His Son, who won forgiveness for the times we fail. Thus assured of

God's love and forgiveness, we can move forward as His children, walking in His ways.

> *Dear God, help me to take another look at my commitment to the work You have given me to do. Keep me from becoming discouraged. Help me to stick with it, but also show me when to step back and allow You to step forward. In Jesus' name. Amen.*

L.T.

A Valentine's Day Gift

*The LORD is close to the brokenhearted
and saves those who are crushed in
spirit. Psalm 34:18*

"I wish we could just skip Valentine's Day this year,"
Jennifer moaned as she signed her name to another card.
She punctuated her comment with a heavy sigh before con-
tinuing to work on her valentines for the school party.

As an 11-year-old, Jennifer was aware that this holiday
celebrated loving relationships. She wasn't in the mood to
celebrate, however, because two of her closest girlfriends
had been avoiding her.

Because I didn't want the holiday to be completely
ruined, I decided to get Jennifer a gift. At a gem and jewelry
show I attended the next day, I noticed a box of polished
stones of various colors and shapes. Each stone had a hook
so it could be worn as a pendant.

I slipped my hand into the mound of cold, smooth
stones. After letting the stones run through my fingers, only
a red heart-shaped stone remained in my hand.

What a great Valentine's Day gift, I thought. But when I
turned the stone over, there was a small indentation where a
piece had broken off. Disappointed, I searched for another
red stone, but I couldn't find one. Holding the stone in my
hand, I wondered what I could do with this beautiful, broken stone.

I remembered Psalm 147:3: "He heals the brokenhearted and binds up their wounds." The significance of this flawed stone became clear to me, and I bought it.

I could hardly wait for Jennifer to come home from school so I could give the pendant to her. When she arrived home, I placed the heart perfect side up, in my daughter's cupped hand. I told her it was my gift to her on this Valentines's Day. I asked her to wear it as a token of my love.

Then I turned the pendant over to expose the broken area. I also asked Jennifer to wear the pendant as a reminder that though there are spots in our hearts that are broken, God knows and He cares. "In fact, God is affected by what affects *you*," I told Jennifer. "He loves you and wants you to remember that He is your dearest and most trusted Friend. And He will never hurt you or leave you."

That day my daughter learned a valuable lesson. She discovered that we live in an imperfect world. People will break off pieces of our heart. And when it happens, it hurts. But God sent His only Son to bind up those broken spots. Through His suffering and death, He won forgiveness for the times we hurt others and for hurts we allow to fester inside ourselves. Through His resurrection, we know that all the broken pieces of our lives will be forgotten in the perfection of our eternal life in heaven.

Thank You, God, that Your gift of gracious love in my Savior Jesus Christ mends the broken pieces of my heart. Amen.

N.O.B.

Invisible Marks

*All these people gave their gifts out of
their wealth; but she out of her poverty
put in all she had to live on. Luke 21:4*

One morning as Mary and I walked along the dirt road
leading from her house to mine, Mary said she wondered if
she would leave any impression on the world. "After all, I'm
certainly no theologian or great thinker," she said. "I don't
even really have a career yet."

Mary had married young. She was barely 16 when her
son was born, and a couple of years later, Lydia arrived.
Mary had entered nurse's training after that, but a divorce
forced her to leave school to work to support herself and the
children.

As we sank down on a log beside the road, Mary's long
red hair brushed against my shoulder. I wanted to reach out
and pull her into my arms, but I knew it wasn't the time for
that. This was a woman to woman talk.

Mary's statement reminded me of my mother, who
never really had a career. I recalled my embarrassment as a
teenager when people asked me what kind of work my
mother did. She had worked many jobs, most of them as a
waitress or as a sales clerk in a department store. She held
none of these positions for more than a few months. But her
coworkers and customers loved my mother. They trusted
her, sought her advice, and came to her with their problems.

When my mother died, there were few people whom

the world would call successful at her funeral. But the woman she had befriended while she waitressed came to the funeral home. She sat in a chair in the corner for a last visit. The young boy next door to whom my mother had given cookies stopped by. And so did the librarian who had loaned my mother every book in the library at least once. They came because my mother had been their friend.

"Mary, look at this," I said as I pointed to tiny squiggly marks in the sandy soil.

"What in the world are those?" she asked.

"I think it's where the earthworms come out during the night," I said. "Evidently they come out, do whatever it is that earthworms do, then leave again before the rest of the world wakes up."

"Why haven't I noticed them before?" she asked.

"Probably because you haven't looked closely enough," I suggested.

I glanced at Mary. "Could that be the reason you think you're not making your mark on the world—because you aren't looking closely enough?" I asked.

She lifted her blue eyes. For the first time that morning, I saw hope and understanding. "What about the smile you give all the customers when they come into the store?" I asked. "That makes a bigger impression than you think. And how about the way people talk to you about their problems? You're making your mark in the world whether you realize it or not.

"People used to come to Grandma Jenny with their problems too," I told Mary.

By now she was smiling. "Have you ever thought about the children that you take to the ball game on Saturdays—

the ones whose parents don't have the time—or the kids at school who know you as the 'class mom'?" I continued.

"All right, all right," she laughed. "I get the message. You know, you're getting more and more like Grandma Jenny yourself!"

Not a bad legacy to follow, I thought.

Lord, help me remember that the world's standards of success differ from Yours. Remind me that my real success comes through Jesus Christ, my Savior, who covered my sins with His perfect sacrifice on the cross. His death makes me clean and acceptable in Your sight. Thank You for putting me in the place You want me and giving me the gifts I need to serve You. In Jesus' name. Amen.

L.T.

When Is a Boo-Boo Not a Boo-Boo?

But He was pierced for our transgressions, He was crushed for our iniquities; the punishment that brought us peace was upon Him, and by His wounds we are healed. Isaiah 53:5

There comes a time when every young lady must try new things—spread her wings and take that first solo flight. And so it happened for Jennifer one Sunday morning when our family overslept and had to rush to get ready for church.

On that particular day, Jennifer had decided to wear a new dress she'd purchased with her own money. She'd also decided that her long hair *had* to be curled. I had agreed to provide the new hairstyle.

Because of the time crunch, I knew I wouldn't have an extra moment to help her. So I did what any other all-American mother would do—I handed the curling iron to my preteen and told her to curl her own hair.

While I quickly applied my makeup, Jennifer was busy wrapping long strands of brown hair around the rod. She'd gotten about halfway done when I heard her scream. I rushed to her side and found the curling iron on the floor, tears in her eyes, and a nasty red burn on her thigh.

"What happened?" I asked as I picked up the hot iron from the carpet. "Are you okay?" (A really dumb question considering the obvious mark of injury.)

"I dropped it," was all Jennifer could say through heart-wrenching sobs.

I held her for a moment, wiped away her tears, then treated the burn. After I finished her hair, we dashed off to church.

During the following weeks, the wound healed, but a telltale scar remained. This prompted my daughter to lament about the ugly mark on her leg.

"Everyone will be able to see this when I wear my bathing suit," she complained. "My whole leg is ruined."

I sympathized with her reaction. I remember thinking that the world would notice the one chicken pox mark on my face. And I was abhorred when a fatty tumor was surgically removed from my leg and left a round, red scar. It's been more than 25 years and it's still there!

I have other scars as well, but no one can see them. They hurt the most because they are engraved deeply on my soul. We all have them because there's no way to escape the bumps and bruises caused by sin, which is part of our world.

But a scar doesn't have to be an ugly reminder of a past sin. It can be a joyous affirmation that our heavenly Father is at work in our lives. The Great Physician knows our hurts. He desires to make us whole again. And He has provided the healing through the actions of His Son on the cross. With that assurance, we can spread our wings and try new things, trusting that our heavenly Father is watching over us.

Lord Jesus, when I consider Your scarred hands and feet, remind me that Your death and resurrection have brought about my eternal healing. Amen.

N.O.B.

Growing with God in Prayer

The prayer of the upright pleases Him.
Proverbs 15:8b

Each night as I put her to bed, Robin and I repeated a common prayer for children, "Now I lay me down to sleep ..." Before we ate, we usually asked the blessing she learned in school, "God is good. God is great ..." The Lord's Prayer was another prayer Robin learned, just as I had in my childhood. No matter the translation, the meaning remains the same: "Our Father in heaven, hallowed be Your name, Your kingdom come, Your will be done on earth as it is in heaven. Give us today our daily bread. Forgive us our debts, as we also have forgiven our debtors. And lead us not into temptation, but deliver us from the evil one" (Matthew 6:9–13).

While most Christians know the words, how many of us really pay attention to what we're saying? I remember a game we played at youth functions when my girls were teens. Everyone sat in a circle and the leader whispered a sentence to one person. That individual whispered the sentence to the next person and so on around the circle. The last person repeated the sentence out loud, but the message usually had changed completely in the trip around the circle. The leader used the game to teach a lesson about gossip, but I believe it also teaches a lesson about prayer.

Have we repeated the Lord's Prayer so often that we don't even think about what we are saying? Or do we repeat the same blessing over our meals until it no longer has meaning?

When we allow children to voice their own prayers, their requests can be surprising. My daughters have prayed for a new puppy and for a swimming pool. They have prayed for an A on a test and for a boy to call. But they also have prayed for a sick friend and for the neighbor next door. Perhaps we as adults could benefit from trying different methods of prayer to revitalize our talks with the Lord.

Why not try a new place to pray instead of the usual bedside, dining room table, or church pew? How about kneeling if you usually sit, or standing with eyes wide open and raised to the heavenly Father if you normally kneel? You could write out prayers or use prayers from a prayer book. You could pray with another person or pray alone.

Prayer is an important part of our spiritual life. It gives us the opportunity to petition God on behalf of ourselves, our friends, and our loved ones. It a source of communication with our heavenly Father. It is an invitation extended to us by God Himself, one we can take full advantage of because of Christ's saving work on the cross.

> *Jesus, thank You for teaching us how to pray. Make me aware of the privilege I have as God's special child to enter His throne room and approach Him with my prayers of thanks, petition, confession, and adoration. Help me to find a new place and time for prayer each day. Amen.*

L.T.

Under Construction

*We will in all things grow up into Him
who is the Head, that is, Christ.
Ephesians 4:15*

*He has made everything beautiful in its
time. Ecclesiastes 3:11*

As we raise children, we see that they are in a perpetual process of growth, constantly under construction.

Jennifer's unpredictable mood swings clearly gave away the fact that she was about to enter adolescence. As she gained a few inches, lost a few pounds, and developed a beautiful figure, Jennifer's mood swings fit the stereotype of an emerging teen.

Although I knew that this was a normal part of maturation, I often wondered if this phase would ever pass and if, in the meanwhile, I would survive.

I think that one of the most rapidly developing parts of preteenagers is their mouth. It seems that Jennifer always has something to say. And the evidence for this fact is twofold. First, she is constantly on the telephone. Second, she invariably has an answer or retort to something I've said or have asked her to do. I particularly dislike this new aspect of our interaction. I don't like to hear her argue, complain about, or question my every request.

Raising a daughter can be a challenge to faith and perseverance. Only the Lord can provide the will and determination to maintain Christian standards for discipline in light of such opposition. Only He can bring my daughter back when she takes off on her own path.

This lesson was brought home to me when I innocently asked Jennifer to clean her room. She was in a particularly foul mood, so she responded, "Why should I? Your room is a mess."

After a long dissertation on why she should obey me and not talk back, I walked into my messy bedroom to put away some laundry. I realized that though she shouldn't have spoken to me like that, Jennifer was right. I wasn't setting a good example for her.

I too am a work in progress. Although I am mature in years, I still have much to learn. I still have plenty of room to grow in the areas of faith, education, communication, and relationships. I am thankful that, throughout my lifetime, God is continually at work in my life to help me grow—mentally, physically, emotionally, and especially spiritually. I would hate to remain a tantrum-throwing 2-year-old or an emotionally immature adolescent my whole life. (Now that's a scary thought!)

God is at work in my heart and life through His Word and sacraments. He is strengthening me and calling me to the fullness of life He has planned for me. Because I am His unique and special creation, conceived by His heart and hand, saved by the blood of His precious Son, God will love me with patience and in abundance. Surely, I can do the same for myself and the ones I love.

Almighty God, You are my Creator. Mold me into the masterpiece You want me to be and help me to never settle for second best. Send Your Holy Spirit to strengthen me and nurture me in the faith so I may grow into Him who is my head—Christ. In His name. Amen.

N.O.B.

Backyard Blessings

So when you give to the needy, do not
announce it with trumpets, as the hyp-
ocrites do in the synagogues and on the
streets, to be honored by men.
Matthew 6:2

Everyone who passed by stopped to admire the
grapevine that edged the path to our home. With proper
pruning, fertilization, and loads of attention, the plant stag-
gered the supports with the weight of its heavy fruit.

After 15-year-old Katie had helped me gather some of
the grapes, I asked her to help clear out some brush in the
backyard. I hoped the job would work off some of her frustration. That morning she had started a volunteer job at a
physical therapy clinic. She had been given the task of filing
patient reports in a back room while her friend was asked to
help the receptionist out front.

I was trying to decide what I could say to comfort Katie
when she called to me. "Mom, look here," she said, pointing
to a familiar form that had carved its way through the dried
grass and leaves. "It's a grapevine. It must have been cut
down before we moved here. It's coming back to life."

She gently freed the vine from surrounding twigs and
followed it to an old stump. Surprisingly, the stump was covered with the same lush grapes that grew on the vine in
front of the house. We sat down on the ground and began
eating the grapes, enjoying their succulent sweetness.

"Isn't it interesting how this vine has kept growing and

flourishing without us even knowing it was here?" I asked.

"Yeah," Katie answered as she lay back on the carpet of leaves. "And I think these grapes taste better than the ones out front."

I watched silently as Katie popped one plump grape after another into her mouth. "You know something, Mom?" she said. "Maybe it's not so bad after all, working in the file room. Whether people can see me working or not, I am still helping the clinic. God sees my labor and He can make it fruitful."

Lord Jesus, send Your Holy Spirit to guide my words and actions to bear fruit for You alone. When I feel unappreciated, remind me that Your sacrifice on the cross for me is my motivation to do my tasks in ways that will bring praise to my Father in heaven. Amen.

L.T.

Good Heart

These commandments that I give you
today are to be upon your hearts.
Impress them on your children. Talk
about them when you sit at home and
when you walk along the road, when you
lie down and when you get up.
Deuteronomy 6:6–7

Brokenhearted over my grandmother's sudden death, I stared out the airport window. Grammy had been a cornerstone of my life. As a child I had visited her often. She demonstrated the importance of Christ through words and actions. I wondered how I would pass on her legacy of faith, honesty, love, and helpfulness.

I walked back to my husband, Mike. All I could think about was Grammy's funeral and how much I would miss her. I knew if I continued to dwell on my loss, I would cry. I needed something to occupy my mind on the flight home.

"I think I'll get a magazine," I told Mike.

"Okay. Let's go," he said as he picked up the magazines he had purchased earlier.

Glancing through the bookstore window, a rack of car magazines caught Mike's attention. "We can't go in with these," he said, pointing to his magazines. "They may not believe we purchased these at another store."

Looking at the cashier, I made eye contact with her and smiled. I took Mike's arm and took a position in line behind the paying customers.

"What are you doing?" he asked me.

"Help you?" the cashier asked in broken English. We stepped to her side of the cash register.

"Yes, ma'am," I said. "I wanted you to know that we came in with these magazines. I didn't want you to think we took them without paying for them."

The woman smiled broadly. Thumping her chest twice with her hand, she said, "Ahh, good heart." She nodded that she understood and waved her hand for us to browse the aisles.

As I walked toward the magazines, my "good" heart skipped a beat, and my eyes filled with tears. I knew God would provide the ways to witness the Christian values Grammy had taught me. And if He would bless my witness in such simple things, how much more He would bless my witness to the saving work of His Son on the cross.

Dear God, thank You for the Christian people You put in my life to provide examples that I can follow. Send Your Holy Spirit to keep me faithful to the standard to which You have called me. Through my words and actions, may I demonstrate Your love and the precious Good News of Jesus, my Savior. In His name. Amen.

N.O.B.

Love Knots

~tie your love together with these ideas

Grow Together

1. **Grow through encouragement.** Slip love notes
   (notes of personal encouragement) into a
   lunch box, notebook, or briefcase. Or mail a
   packet of love notes to a child or mother who
   lives far away. Each note could be placed in a
   separate envelope and titled, "Monday,"
   "Tuesday," or "When you feel blue," etc.
   Include favorite Bible verses, hymn verses, or
   mention specific ways you have prayed for your
   daughter or mother.

2. **Grow through remembering.** Record your
   daughter or mother on audio- or videocassette
   as she describes major milestones in her life.
   Such events might include a special church
   service, a youth event or women's retreat, a
   first date or school dance, a job interview, or
   the funniest thing that ever happened to her. If
   your mother is deceased, write down or record
   special events she told you about. Add to this
   "diary" and pass it down to each generation.

3. **Grow through doing.** Teach your daughter
   how to do household jobs such as ironing,

mopping the floor, cleaning the toilet, and cutting the grass. Children learn more by doing than by watching. While working together, discuss why these tasks are necessary for dorm life, independent living, and/or married life. Grandmother can add interest and perspective by sharing how everyday tasks have changed through the years. In addition to these tasks, model for your daughter the importance of daily time with God through study of His Word and in prayer. You might include her in your devotional time, begin regular family devotions, or purchase a devotional book and Bible for her personal use.

4. **Grow through sound health practices.** Talk about nutrition, the need for checkups, and the importance of exercise. Begin an exercise program together such as walking or aerobics. Take advantage of programs at your local hospital such as informational classes, blood pressure screening, or free inoculations. Discuss the unique gifts God has given us in our bodies and the many ways He provides for us to maintain good health.

5. **Grow through giving.** Teach your daughter how to care for a baby, then volunteer to work in the church nursery together. Or give of your time at a homeless shelter, assisted care facility, or women's shelter. Before you begin work, ask God to bless your service and make you wit-

nesses of His good gifts, especially the gift of Jesus.

6. **Grow through planning**. Occasionally allow your daughter to help write checks for family expenses. This will help educate her about budgeting and financial planning. Work together to identify ways expenses can be cut. Decide on a special project for the savings you've created, such as sponsoring a missionary or contributing to a special project at church or school.

7. **Grow through sharing.** Write a letter to your mother or daughter telling her how proud you are that she's your mother or daughter. Name specific ways in which God has made her a blessing to you.

8. **Grow through learning.** Ask your daughter to share her special gifts with you. She might teach you to dance, to surf the Internet, or to enjoy a new craft. Your willingness to learn and admit imperfection will help your daughter become secure in her abilities, in her efforts to try new things, and even in her ability to handle failure. Praise each other for the gifts God has given each of you.

9. **Grow through communication.** Practice good listening skills. Give your full attention to the speaker and make eye contact with the audience. Respect each other by not interrupting.

Ask open-ended questions to maintain the conversation. Discuss how these techniques will strengthen communication skills in all relationships. Discuss how we employ these techniques in our relationship with God.

10. **Grow through preparation.** Play "What If." For example, ask, "What if I were supposed to meet you after the movies, and I didn't show up? What would you do?" This game encourages your daughter to develop safe, common-sense solutions in a nonthreatening environment. Remind her that God is always with her and will help her remember these solutions should she ever find herself in a disturbing situation. The situations don't always have to be frightening. Include some fun scenarios to keep the game light.

FAITH

Prayer

Dear God,

Sometimes it seems impossible to live out my faith. The neighbor next door complains, and I get angry. My daughter's best friend betrays her, her heart breaks, and so does mine. It looks as though my mother will not recover from her illness, and we both despair. The enemy knows my weak spots and scores a direct hit.

Lord, remind me that through faith I am Your beloved child. You will guide me through the trials and temptations of life. You will send Your Holy Spirit to strengthen me and keep me in the true faith.

Remind me that faith is more than a feeling. A living faith leads to action. Move me to reach out and tell others of Your love and mercy in Jesus Christ. Move me to reach down and help someone up. Move me to reach up and offer You not only my petitions, but my praise.

You know the challenges a mother and daughter face. And You know how our faith falters. Give us the ability to trust each other just as, in faith, You have given us the ability to trust You. In Jesus' name. Amen.

God Loves Hamsters Too

*I tell you the truth, unless you change and
become like little children, you will never
enter the kingdom of heaven.*
Matthew 18:3

"Mommy, Mommy, come quick!" Jennifer yelled from her bedroom.

I ran across the house and found her standing in front of the hamster cage.

Is the hamster dead? I thought.

"What's the matter?" I asked as my eyes searched the cage for a lifeless form.

"He's gone—Oreo's gone!" Jennifer wailed.

"Gone? How could he get out? Didn't you close the latch?" I asked.

Jennifer assured me that the cage had been locked securely. She also reminded me of Oreo's favorite pastime, which was climbing atop his food dish so he could push the door open. That's why we'd nicknamed him Houdini.

We spent the next hour on our hands and knees, searching for the rascally rodent. We looked under the bed, moved each piece of furniture, and rummaged through every box in Jennifer's messy closet. Then we broadened our search to the hallway, the bathroom, and eventually to Matthew's room. There was no escape artist in sight.

Periodically throughout the day, we continued our quest to find Oreo. Nasty visions played in my mind of gnawed clothing or wiring. We had to find my daughter's pet before it got hurt and before Jennifer grew more upset.

By mid-afternoon I had given up and started to prepare dinner. Jennifer recognized my surrender and came into the kitchen. "Mommy, we can't give up. We need to pray," she said matter-of-factly. So we prayed that God would bring her hamster out of hiding.

I couldn't help but wonder what would happen. Had it been a good idea to pray for such a trivial thing? Surely God had more important matters to think about than a little lost animal.

That night when I tucked Jennifer into bed, she once again asked the Lord to help us find Oreo. "And thank You, God, for taking care of him while he's loose. I know You love him too. Amen," Jennifer prayed in conclusion. She kissed me goodnight, closed her eyes, and drifted off to sleep.

I, however, wondered how I would get to sleep knowing that a rodent was on the loose. I thought about what would happen if Oreo got outside. (God forbid!) Or what would happen if the dog found him while we were sleep. (Yuck, too gruesome to even think about.) And what would happen if … As I lay in bed listening to the silence of the night, I wondered again if God would answer my daughter's plea.

Then I heard a noise near my head. Because I knew the dog was in the living room with my husband, I got scared. *What could it be?* The rustling came again. I quickly turned on the light. Looking toward the noise, I saw two beady eyes staring back at me. It was Oreo!

He was as surprised as I was and sat motionless on the

nightstand. I scooped him up in my hands and triumphantly marched him back to his cage. I woke Jennifer and explained the whole story to her.

"See, I told you," Jennifer scolded me.

"Told me what?" I asked.

"I told you that God would find him. And He did."

I smiled. She was right. How foolish of me to think that I couldn't "bother" God with small, everyday requests. And how wonderful that the Creator had shown me all of this because of a little girl's *big* faith.

Dear God, thank You that Your loving care extends to all creatures great and small. You demonstrate this care when You watch over the sparrows (and hamsters), but more important, You lavished this care on me when You came to me when I was lost, sending Your Holy Spirit to work faith in Jesus in my heart. You brought me into Your family through Baptism. Thank You. In my Savior's precious name. Amen.

N.O.B.

Have You Met Linda?

*Make every effort to add to your faith
goodness; and to goodness, knowledge;
and to knowledge, self-control; and to
self-control, perseverance; and to perseverance, godliness; and to godliness,
brotherly kindness; and to brotherly kindness, love. 2 Peter 1:5–7*

I did not have the opportunity to attend college after
high school. Instead, I enrolled in a business college at night
so I could work during the day to help pay household
expenses for my mother and my teenage brother. When I
had the opportunity to attend college later in life, I was
thrilled.

I wanted to go to college to gain more knowledge, not
because it was required. But there was a problem. My daughter Katie attended the same college. Although she was a
high school senior, she was taking advanced courses at the
college. Knowing teens as I did, I realized meeting Mom in
the halls might make life uncomfortable for my daughter.

"If we meet on campus, I'll act like I don't know you," I
told Katie. "I won't even look in your direction."

Katie smiled sheepishly. She never would have admitted
it for fear of hurting my feelings, but I knew she was grateful. I hadn't forgotten what it was like to have parents
around when you were trying to be independent. It could
make things awkward, especially where young men were
concerned.

For the next six or eight weeks, we both had fun, earned good grades, made new friends, and got along fine—separately. We ignored each other at school. In fact, I hardly ever saw Katie. I was beginning to wonder if she watched for me so she could head in the opposite direction.

With each passing day, I was accepted more and more by the younger students. Making friends was easy as we worked together on class projects or discussed pre-test jitters while waiting for class to start.

One day I was looking over an essay for a friend of mine. We were sitting on a bench outside our classroom. As I jotted a few suggestions in the margins, I heard him say, "Hi, Katie. Come sit down. Class hasn't started yet, and Linda is trying to pound some sense into my head about writing." I looked up just as he said, "This is one woman we all need to know. Have you two met?"

"Uh ... uh," I stammered, not sure of what to say.

"Yes, we met quite some time ago," Katie said, smiling at me with an amused look in her eyes. "In fact, I guess we've been friends for about seventeen years now, wouldn't you say ... Mom?"

"Mo ... Mom?" he sputtered as we both burst out laughing.

The young man must have thought we had lost our minds.

I think we both learned a valuable lesson that day about our individual strengths and trust in each other. Katie learned to view my maturity and the knowledge I had from my life experiences with newly appreciative eyes. I learned to trust Katie's ability to adjust to attending school with her mother.

Throughout the school year, we learned many lessons from the new situations in which we found ourselves. God gave us a new appreciation for each other and sent His Holy Spirit to add extra measures of goodness, knowledge, perseverance, and self-control to our faith.

Dear God, make me more aware of the many strengths and abilities You have given to me and to those I love. Continue to strengthen my faith and trust in You. Send Your Holy Spirit to add goodness, knowledge, self-control, perseverance, godliness, kindness, and love to my repertoire. Thank You for the forgiveness Your Son won for me for the times when I avoid letting others see that I believe in You. In Jesus' name. Amen.

L.T.

Angels Watching over Me

Now faith is being sure of what we hope
for and certain of what we do not see.
Hebrews 11:1

When my mother called long-distance one Saturday to
tell me that my grandfather had died, I was overwhelmed
with grief. Pop Pop had been my friend, my confidant, and a
source of encouragement since I was a child. Although he
was almost 90 years old and sick with pneumonia, I still
wasn't prepared to lose him.

Over the past five years, I had shared my faith with
him.

"Pop Pop," I'd say, "I want you to be there for me when
I get to heaven." I told him all about Jesus and the wonderful gift of salvation. I knew that the Bible said the only way
to get to heaven is through Jesus. Did my grandfather
believe this to be true? I needed to know.

As the day progressed, I prepared for our family to
attend Pop Pop's funeral. We would leave in a few days.
Tears flowed as I grieved over his death. Had the Lord used
my words to make a difference in my grandfather's life?
Would he be there with Jesus to greet me when I reached
heaven's gate?

When I prayed that evening, I asked God to protect us
as we traveled to New Jersey. I asked Him to comfort me
and to show me that His angels had watched over my
beloved grandfather.

The next morning we attended church. Jennifer had been asked to sing a solo verse as a portion of the song that the children's choir was singing that morning. As she took her place in front of the choir, I wondered if she could remain composed enough to sing.

Before the music began, Jennifer stepped up to the microphone and announced, "I'd like to dedicate this song to my great-grandfather who died yesterday. I know he's in heaven with Jesus and that the angels watched over him."

The music started and my sweet daughter sang, "All night, all day, angels watchin' over me, my Lord." Joy flooded my spirit as I felt the peace of God surround me. If God could arrange for Jennifer to sing this song the day after her great-grandfather died, then surely He could have used me to share the message of salvation with Pop Pop.

Tears of thanksgiving flowed as I listened to my daughter sing. I knew that Pop Pop would be at my Savior's side when I reached heaven's gate.

O God, thank You for comforting me when I am in the valley of despair. Remind me that You have planned for my salvation and completed that plan in the Person of Your Son, Jesus. Help me to rest assured that His death and resurrection ensure forgiveness of sins and life eternal. Use my words and actions to communicate this Good News to other, especially to my family. In my Savior's name. Amen.

N.O.B.

Faith in His Future

"For I know the plans I have for you,"
declares the LORD, "plans to prosper you
and not to harm you, plans to give you
hope and a future." Jeremiah 29:11

There were times that I wondered if I was supposed to be a writer. I dreamed of spending my days writing, letting my imagination take me to other worlds, having people wait anxiously for my next book. But it didn't seem to be working out as I had dreamed. I had to work a full-time job and juggle my writing around responsibilities at work and at home. It wasn't as much fun as I had thought it would be.

But deep inside, I knew this wasn't like other "things" I wanted in my life. It wasn't a passing fancy. It was a gift from God, something He wanted me to use. Knowing this didn't make it any easier. For one whole year, I received nothing but rejection slips. After a while, it seemed foolish to get up at 4 A.M. every morning to spend time writing things that apparently no one wanted to read.

Katie was in kindergarten during these early days in my writing career. I remember taking her to see a musical sponsored by the local arts council. The dancers captivated her. "Mommy, someday I'm going to be a wonderful dancer," she said when we returned home. "I'll be rich and famous. Just wait and see!"

"You certainly will, if that's what God has planned for you," I told her, laughing as she danced around the room.

Watching her youth and exuberance, I was sure Katie could do whatever she set her mind to do. *I only wish I were that sure about myself,* I thought.

As the years passed, my writing began to sell. By that time, Katie was in third grade and had decided that she would be an astronaut. "I'm going to be on all the televisions and in all the newspapers when I grow up. I'll be the first woman to walk on Mars. Just wait and see!" she said.

"Perhaps you will," I told her, "if that's God's plan." Seeing the dreams in her shining eyes, I wanted the same confidence.

When I became a contributing editor with *Guideposts*, Katie was entering junior high. By then she was certain she would be a lawyer. "Mama, I'll be the best lawyer ever. I'll make lots of money, and people will call me from everywhere to take their cases. Just wait and see!" she said.

"I'll pray for you," I told her. "After all, dreams can come true." But I knew that fulfilling those dreams wouldn't be easy.

I started writing books about the same time Katie started high school. That's when she began seriously to question the future. She was no longer sure about what she wanted to do. "Maybe ... I don't know ... if I wait, maybe I'll see ..."

"Perhaps that's best," I told her. *She's searching, Lord, please guide her,* I prayed.

The years flew by. She was in college and the future she'd dreamt about all her life was right around the corner. And she was even less certain. She talked to professors, took compatibility tests, tried different courses, and worried. "Mom, I just don't know any longer. I'm not sure ... it's hard to see ... maybe it's safer to wait."

"God will guide you," I told her, but I knew she needed to learn that for herself. It took me a long time to become assured that I was doing what God had planned for me to do.

No one can teach us to follow our dreams, we have to learn to follow them ourselves. While we can learn from the wisdom and experience of others, only God can lead us in the way He has planned for us.

Father, guide me to the path, the future, You have planned for me. Make me a fruitful member of Your family as I complete the tasks You place before me. Thank You for the wonderful assurance that because of Jesus, who redeemed me with His precious blood, I have a place in Your kingdom. Amen.

L.T.

Communication 101

When I was a child, I talked like a child,
I thought like a child, I reasoned like a
child. When I became a man, I put child-
ish ways behind me. 1 Corinthians 13:11

When Jennifer was about 3 years old, she loved to draw
and color. Because she often saw me writing, she decided to
add words to her pictures. Taking a jumbo crayon in her
chubby little hand, she scribbled unintelligible letters on her
paper.

One day she decided to make me a card. She sat at the
kitchen table to draw her picture and color it. Inside, she
wrote a beautifully scripted, heartfelt message to me—in
scribbles. After adding several pretty red flowers on the back
of the card, my little girl finished her project. She put away
her crayons and brought her work of art to me.

"Here, Mommy," she said as she proudly handed me the
homemade card. "This is for you." She smiled broadly, then
hugged my legs.

"Thank you," I replied as I bent over to give her a kiss.
"This is beautiful!"

"Open it up," my daughter instructed.

I opened the card and saw the page of scribbles.

"Do you know what it says?" Jennifer asked hopefully.

Is this a trick question? I wondered. Of course I couldn't
understand my preschooler's attempt at writing. *Does she
expect me to pretend to read it? Lord, help!* After all her hard

work, I didn't want to insult her good intentions. I knew what to do.

"This is so special, and I know you spent a lot of time thinking about what you wanted to say. It would mean a great deal to me if you would read it," I said.

Jennifer's eyes sparkled as she took the card and opened it so she could read her message to me. Although her scribbles didn't make sense to me, she knew exactly what they said. She read the whole page aloud.

This incident made me wonder about how *I* communicate. Are my attempts to communicate sometimes childish and unclear to others? Although I may think I put my best foot forward, I sometimes wind up with my foot in my mouth!

And what about my communication with my heavenly Father? My prayers are sometimes no more clear than a 3-year-old's scribbles. In the busyness of my day or the weakness of the moment, I wonder if my heavenly Father has any idea what I'm trying to say.

The good news, of course, is that God always understands my attempts to communicate. Just as I gladly received my daughter's card, God joyfully receives our efforts to communicate.

When I was a young Christian, I didn't know how to talk to or listen to God. But as I've matured, the Holy Spirit has helped me learn to communicate with God through Bible study and prayer. I've also learned to express myself to others so they will know that I'm a Christian.

I'm still growing in faith. Just as Jennifer eventually learned to write "real" words and to arrange them in sentences that made sense, I too am in a learning process. As the years pass, I will continue to put childish ways behind me as the Holy Spirit is at work in my heart and life to put into practice God's teachings. My daughter and I will continue to grow together as we seek the One who knows our thoughts before we even utter or write a word.

Almighty God, instill in me a desire to learn more from You. As I grow in faith, guide me to be an effective witness so I can communicate Your merciful actions with the people I meet. In my Savior's name. Amen.

N.O.B.

Your People Will Be My People

*"Don't urge me to leave you or to turn
back from you. Where you go I will go,
and where you stay I will stay. Your people will be my people and your God my
God." Ruth 1:16*

The day Christy, our son's fiancée, was baptized was a
special celebration. I was proud of Christy. She had confessed Christ as her Savior, and as our pastor lifted her head
from the baptismal water, gratefulness filled my heart that
she and Andy would live their lives committed to serving
and obeying God.

As the pastor turned her toward us, Andy walked forward to light a candle at the altar, symbolizing the new faith
of his young bride-to-be. I marveled at the emotions clearly
displayed on Christy's face. I rejoiced at God's promises fulfilled, the hopes and dreams for the future answered, and
the gift of faith.

While I celebrated the faith in Jesus that God had
given to Christy, I also rejoiced at the faith He had given
her in this new church family, as well as her new family by
marriage. She trusted the new relationships, even with all
the turns and twists, sisters and brothers, nieces and
nephews. She also had faith in me as her mother-in-law.

What would the coming days, months, and years hold for us?
I wondered. I knew each of us—the church, the family, me—

would fail Christy at times. We are sinners and we cannot escape that reality here on earth. While I couldn't do anything about the members of the church or the other members of the family, I could ask God to direct the role I would play in her life. How could I learn to be a good mother-in-law?

I thought of Ruth and her mother-in-law, Naomi. How did Naomi manage to elicit such faithfulness and love from her daughters-in-law? When Naomi tried to send both of them back to their mothers, they loved her so much that they protested vigorously. Orpah wept, but Naomi finally persuaded her to leave. Ruth, however, flatly refused to go. The Bible says, "Ruth clung to her" (Ruth 1:14).

Perhaps her daughters-in-law loved her because they were important to Naomi, and she let them know it. If the truth were known, she really needed both young women to stay with her, but she requested they leave because she knew it would be better for them. But Naomi didn't insist on having her way. She gave them options and let them make their own decisions. Orpah and Ruth made different decisions, but Naomi treated those decisions with equal respect. She loved them, therefore, they loved her.

As the baptismal service ended, the congregation and family surrounded Andy and Christy, wishing them well. *Today has been a good day,* I thought, *but not all the days in the lives of this congregation or this family will go so well. Some will be better. Some will be worse. There will be joyful reunions and holiday gatherings, but there also will be moments of pain and hurt feelings.* "Lord," I prayed, "as this beautiful young woman enters our church family and our family, help us to treat her with the love and respect that You extend so graciously to us."

Father God, thank You for the gift of new life for Jesus'
sake and for feelings of love. Help me to be strong when
the times of pain or disappointment come and to trust
in the power of Your saving grace. Help me to fulfill
the role I have been given within my family with grace,
forgiveness, and love. In Jesus' name. Amen.

L.T.

The Sound of Silence

Let the wise listen and add to their
learning. Proverbs 1:5

When Jennifer was a preschooler, we often played outside together and enjoyed the beautiful Florida sunshine.
Sometimes I pushed her on the swing or I watched her ride
her tricycle. Other times we took a walk or just amused ourselves in the backyard.

One morning while we were outside, I noticed that
Jennifer had stopped playing and was standing perfectly still.
"What's the matter?" I asked.

With wide-open eyes, she turned to look at me. "What's
that sound?" she asked.

I listened. I could hear a truck applying its brakes as it
approached the stop sign nearby. "It's the squeaky brakes on
a truck," I said.

"No," Jennifer replied, "not that noise. Listen."

I listened again. I heard the typical neighborhood noises: dogs barking, cars starting, kids playing. Nothing seemed
out of the ordinary.

"There it goes again!" Jennifer exclaimed.

I strained to hear this mysterious sound. Standing
motionless next to Jennifer, I tuned out the everyday world-
ly noises and waited.

Rat-a-tat-tat, rat-a-tat-tat.

"Did you hear it?" Jennifer asked excitedly.

"Yes! It's a woodpecker," I said. "Let's go find him." We

walked to the front yard and saw a red-headed woodpecker tapping his beak on the telephone pole. We stood there, transfixed by the bird's repetitive attempts to find food.

While we watched our noisy, little friend, I began to hear things I hadn't noticed before. I heard the far-off wail of a train whistle. Then the twittering of birds in a melodic symphony filled my ears while a gentle breeze rustled the leaves in our live oak tree. The noises were delightful.

If I hadn't lingered and carefully listened, I would have missed a special moment with my daughter—and with God. This made me wonder how many times I have missed the still small voice of God because I let the world's noises drown Him out.

What do you hear—the world or the whispers of God? Take time today to listen to the soft, loving voice of God in His Word. He will tell you of His love for you and the forgiveness that you have for Jesus' sake.

Lord, remind me that tuning out the world often helps me tune in to You. Send Your Holy Spirit to urge me daily to spend time with You as I read my Bible, meditate on Your Word, and speak with You in prayer. Focus me on the actions of Jesus that have made me Your precious daughter. In His name. Amen.

N.O.B.

Keep the Home Fires Burning

The LORD will be your everlasting light.
Isaiah 60:19b

Six-year-old Robin wasn't feeling too well that winter morning. She had a slight fever and the sniffles so I closed the heavy living room drapes to shut out the cold, brought her some medicine, and settled her on the couch in front of the television.

"I've always heard that a day of cartoons every now and then is good for little girls," I told her, laughing a little. "It makes them feel better!"

As I pulled a pale pink comforter up under her chin, she smiled and snuggled into the fluffy pillows I had placed behind her back.

I wish it were that simple for me, I thought. *If only a day of cartoons would make me feel better.*

It seemed like everything that could go wrong had gone wrong in the last few days. The refrigerator had stopped cooling, and two of the burners on the stove had stopped heating. There were constant detours around sawhorses and buckets of nails, signs of our constant efforts at remodeling. Besides that, winter was approaching and we still hadn't been able to afford the gas furnace we had promised ourselves last year. That meant another year of black smoke pouring from the door of the wood-fired heater, logs stacked in the corner, and soot on the curtains.

As I watched Robin burrow into the pillows, I wanted to join her.

Robin hardly moved from the couch. At lunchtime, I brought a cup of soup to her living room sickbed. After drinking the warm broth, she sat up, propped her pillows around her, and began to position her Barbie dolls among the folds of the comforter. I could tell she was beginning to feel better.

As night approached and I began to close up the house, Robin decided to help me bring in some kindling for the heater. Apparently she had had enough of the couch and was ready for some fresh air. Because her fever was gone and the sniffles had disappeared, I told her it would be all right. When we stepped out into the darkening yard, Robin grew serious. "Mama, didn't the sun come up today?" she asked as she looked at the stars that were beginning to peak through the clouds.

"Of course the sun came up," I assured her, smiling at the unusual question. "In fact, the day was nice and sunny."

Then I understood why she had asked the question. She had been stuck behind the closed drapes all day. She hadn't seen the bright sunshine. "You were feeling too bad to notice," I told her.

"Oh, that's good!" she said with a relieved giggle as she reached down to pick up the sticks of pine. "I sure am glad the sun didn't stop shining."

I gathered an armload of smaller wood to start the heavier logs burning. We hurried inside the house with our fuel for the next morning's fire.

After the girls had gone to bed, I pulled my rocking chair closer to the heater and listened to the wind howling outside the window. The temperature outside had dropped at least 10 degrees since we had brought in the kindling. It was warm beside the heater, though. All I wanted was to relax and let the concerns melt away with the cold, but my thoughts wouldn't leave me alone.

Robin had helped fuel more than the heater—she had fueled something deep inside with her words. How many times I had missed God's blessings because I had draped myself with self-pity and blocked out His light. I actually had many reasons to be thankful ... and one of them was being able to sit beside that aged wood heater. There were many people huddled on street corners and over sewer grates trying to keep from freezing. I had been fussing about needing to gather wood when I should have been grateful that I had access to fuel for the fire that was toasting my toes.

When we allow ourselves to be blinded by insignificant problems, we miss God's sunshine gleaming brightly all around us. We fail to be warmed by the Light of the world, who went to the cross and rose from the dead to take care of our biggest problem—sin and the separation from God that it caused. Like Robin, I sure am glad He's shining even when I'm not looking.

Teach me, Lord, to see Your light. Help me to point others to Your light as well. In Jesus' name. Amen.

L.T.

He Answers All Prayers

*Ask and it will be given to you; seek and
you will find; knock and the door will be
opened to you. For everyone who asks
receives; he who seeks finds; and to him
who knocks, the door will be opened.*
Matthew 7:7–8

It was Labor Day and I'd planned to relax. I puttered
around the kitchen and asked Jennifer to help with the
dishes. After leaving to get her a clean towel, I returned to
see our miniature poodle eating something.

"Jennifer," I asked, "did you give Suzy something to eat?"

"No," she answered.

We dashed over to Suzy and found her chewing a vita-
min E capsule that must have rolled off the counter when
Jennifer moved the dishes. After throwing it out, I noticed
that my other pill was missing. Since it was a prescription
drug, I frantically began to search for it. I knew our beloved
pet could die from ingesting my pill. All I could think of
was the fact that this was a holiday and the vet's office was
closed.

I called our vet at his home, but I didn't get an answer. I
left a message on his machine and called our groomer. She
wasn't home either.

"We need to pray," I told Jennifer and her brother. I
asked God to guide me and to protect our dog. As I said
amen, I had an idea. Even though I hadn't been able to reach
my vet at home, the vet's office should have someone on call.

Then the phone rang. Our vet had received my message and said that the pill Suzy ate wouldn't have any adverse effects on her. Relieved, I thanked him and told the kids the good news.

Returning to the kitchen, I noticed the Scripture passage on my daily devotional calendar. It read, "The effectual fervent prayer of a righteous man availeth much" (James 5:16 KJV).

It sure does, I thought. Even prayers for a poodle!

Lord, thank You for Your guidance, Your intervention, Your protection, and Your healing each day, even for the animals You created. Thank You for healing us from the deadly sickness of sin through Jesus' saving work. Amen.

N.O.B.

You'll Always Be My Father

*You are my Father, my God,
the Rock my Savior. Psalm 89:26b*

I never knew my real father. He left my mother when
my brother, Dan, was a newborn and I was 2 or 3 years old.
My mother remarried, but my stepfather was far from being
a father-figure. I always had a deep longing to find my biological father.

After a long search, I located my uncle, and he arranged
a meeting between me and my father. Of course, he had
another family now that knew nothing about my brother
and me, but that didn't bother me. I didn't want to upset
anyone. I simply wanted to meet the man who had been
responsible for bringing me into the world.

Before we could meet, however, my father became ill,
had a heart attack, and died. Because I didn't officially exist,
my biological uncle didn't notify me until several weeks
after the funeral. Upon hearing the news, I stood there—a
middle-aged woman in front of a sink of dirty dishes—
thinking about a father I'd never known. What would have
happened if we had met? Would he have been glad to see
me? Or would he simply have brushed me off as an inconve-
nience?

My granddaughter Lydia spent the night with me that
night. I smiled as she picked out letters on my computer
keyboard. Her red hair reminded me so much of her mother,
Mary. Light from the overhead lamp caressed the auburn

strands that seemed to float around her head as she concentrated on the screen. The scene made me think of a time many years before when I was washing dishes. Mary was about 2 years old at the time. The same red curls had framed her face.

Mary was a cherub of a child, but like all children, she could be difficult at times. That morning just happened to be one of those times. It seemed she was doing everything she could to prevent me from washing dishes. She pulled at my skirt and got under my feet while I scrubbed the dishes with a soapy sponge.

The hot water felt good to my cold hands that morning. The day had started on a downbeat when I received news that my mother was ill. The illness wasn't serious, but it was enough to make me wonder if I needed to be with her. Then when I checked the mail, I found three past due notices. All of this had topped off the harsh words my husband had spoken to me before he left for work. But all Mary knew was that she wanted some loving. Failing to get my attention, she wrapped her arms around my knees and said fervently, "You'll always be my mommy!"

A laugh slipped out as I let the soapy sponge fall back into the water. I gathered my daughter up in my arms. She didn't seem to mind that my hands were still wet or that soap bubbles tickled her nose. "You're right, honey," I told her. "I will always be your mommy!"

Giggling, we both sank down into a chair in the living room. She snuggled into my lap and relaxed, satisfied because she had my attention. She was secure in the knowledge that I was really there for her for the first time that morning.

Now as I looked at Lydia, I could see that I hadn't needed to worry about the problems that had seemed to bombard me that morning. My mother recovered, the bills were paid, and my husband picked a rose from the garden and brought it in to me when he came home that evening. Even if I'd had to buy flowers for my husband, or the bills hadn't been paid, or if my mother hadn't recovered, God would have been there for me.

With the death of the man whom I'd wanted to call *Father*, I knew I'd never be able to rely on the love of an earthly father. I'd never feel his arms around me or hear his words of comfort. But knowing that I would always be my daughter's mommy, even with all my human weaknesses, helped me understand how much more I could depend on my heavenly Father's grace and love to sustain me. Even with all His responsibilities, I knew that my heavenly Father would drop everything like a soapy sponge when I needed Him. He had sent His only Son to win the forgiveness for my sin that assured me of this loving relationship. Because of this, I have the privilege of calling God *Father!*

Lord, enable me to say with all the love and faith of a child that You will always be my Father! In Jesus' name. Amen.

L.T.

Bedtime Rescue

For He will command His angels concerning you to guard you in all your ways. Psalm 91:11

It was about midnight when my infant daughter, Jennifer, was finally settling down for bed. While I slowly rocked her, I marveled at her cherub-like face. Her rosy cheek lay against my arm as I cuddled her close. She smelled so good after her evening bath that I couldn't resist kissing her once again on her silky brown hair. Eyes closed, she looked so peaceful and beautiful.

Softly singing a lullaby, I watched her as she slept. *I wish I could sleep so peacefully,* I thought. Exhausted from another long day, I longed to crawl into bed for a good night's sleep.

I rose from the rocking chair and carried Jennifer to her crib. Gently pulling a pink blanket over her, I prayed, "God, watch over my baby and keep her safe throughout the night. Please place your guardian angels around her." I quietly left her room and walked to the master bedroom, which was at the other side of our ranch-style home.

After checking that the baby monitor was on, I thankfully crawled into bed. My husband, Mike, was already asleep.

The room was dark and the house quiet. Because of the baby monitor, I heard Jennifer move in her crib. I was always glad to hear her sigh or shift position. After almost losing my precious daughter because of premature labor, I remained anxious, even though she was perfectly healthy.

Night after night I would lie awake, listening intently to the monitor. *Is she all right?* I would wonder. *Is she breathing?*

If I awoke in the middle of the night, I would slip out of bed, tiptoe into her room, and check on her. It was no wonder I was exhausted.

Tonight was no exception. I tried to relax, but I tossed and turned. *This is ridiculous,* I thought as I lay there wide awake. *Either I need a sleeping pill or a miracle. I can't go on like this.*

Suddenly I heard a noise from the other side of the house.

"Mike, wake up," I frantically whispered as I elbowed my husband. "I hear something."

Fear gripped me, and I could barely move. Both Jennifer and our 6-year-old son were asleep at that end of the house. *I know the windows are shut and the doors are locked,* I reasoned. *How could someone get inside?*

I roused Mike from his sleep and forced out the words, "Did you hear that?"

"No," he said.

"Listen," I said and held my breath, waiting to hear the sound again.

"I don't hear anything. Go back to sleep," my husband responded.

Sleep? I thought. *How could he suggest that I sleep?* I was ready to get out of bed, grab the baseball bat, and head for my children's rooms. Instead, however, I prayed.

Slowly, a warm sense of peace and well-being washed over my tired body. I knew that my trust was not in my ability to protect my daughter and my son, but in my heavenly

Father's ability. He would watch over us all and keep us safe. I knew that His guardian angels surrounded us.

As I drifted off to sleep, I knew my daughter would be safe throughout the night and that I would awake refreshed and ready to enjoy a new day.

Dear God, thank You for Your protection, both day and night. I know I have nothing to fear because Jesus has conquered sin and death itself for me and for my daughter. Through Baptism, we are Your precious daughters, and You have promised to be with us always. In Jesus' name. Amen.

N.O.B.

The Shiny Side

I, even I, am He who blots out your
transgressions, for My own sake, and
remembers your sins no more.
Isaiah 43:25

As a young Christian mother, I wondered sometimes if God really "remembered our sins no more." *I know He forgives,* I told myself, *but does He really forget? Or does He still see the stain?*

One day when Katie was about 2 years old, we were sitting in a doctor's waiting room. I tried to interest her in a children's book, but it was no use. She was entranced by the trash can in the corner.

As a mother, that trash receptacle represented only one thing: germs. It might look clean on the outside, but I knew what kind of mess was on the inside. To Katie, the tall, round metal container was an object of wonder. She pointed at it excitedly and repeatedly said, "Robot! Robot!" No amount of motherly words could persuade her that it was not a robot. She knew that it was.

When the nurse called Katie's name and we walked down the hall, I caught myself glancing backward. I wouldn't have been surprised if the "robot" trash can had lit up, started beeping, and turned to follow us.

As I looked at Katie racing ahead of me, I thought about God's forgiveness. It's like that trash can. When God empties our lives of the sin we commit, it's gone. It doesn't keep coming back. He washes us in the blood of His Son and sets us back out to do His work. And He empties our "trash" every time we ask for forgiveness.

But God's saving action is even better than that shiny trash can. The smelly refuse spends many years in a trash dump, but God completely forgets our sins. And the trash may stain the inside of the trash can or leave a residue. Not so when God washes us. The waters of Baptism completely remove the stain of sin. God looks at us and sees the perfection of His Son.

Thank You, Lord, for loving me enough to make me shiny and beautiful in the blood of Your Son. Help me to live a shiny life so others can see Your glory. In Jesus' name. Amen.

L.T.

"I Need a Spoon"

O God, Thou art my God; early will I
seek Thee: My soul thirsteth for Thee.
Psalm 63:1 (KJV)

"Here I am! I stand at the door and
knock. If anyone hears my voice and
opens the door, I will come in and eat
with him, and he with Me."
Revelation 3:20

It was a cold December morning, and I was busy in the kitchen getting breakfast ready. Two-year-old Jennifer sat patiently in her high chair. While she sipped on her cup of juice, she twirled strands of brown hair around her finger and quietly watched my every move.

"Are you hungry?" I asked my little girl. Still sleepy, she nodded her head and continued to wait for me to finish preparing her food.

"Here you go," I said as I placed the bowl of oatmeal in front of her. I tied her bib around her neck, then busied myself once again with my kitchen duties.

While washing the dishes, I realized that Jennifer was staring at me. She wasn't eating her breakfast.

"Why aren't you eating?" I asked. "Is it too hot?"

"I need a spoon," she replied matter-of-factly.

I looked at the high chair tray. Sure enough, there was no spoon. I couldn't believe I had forgotten to give one to her. But I was even more amazed that my daughter sat with the bowl in front of her and never said anything.

This incident reminded me of how I sometimes fail to feed myself spiritually. Since I'm a typical busy mom, I find it difficult to make time for regular Bible study and prayer.

Like Jennifer's oatmeal, my Bible sits on the table— right in front of me. All I have to do is open it and read so the Holy Spirit can feed me with the words of life. But it's not that easy, is it? Human nature takes over, and the many demands on my time get in the way. The Bible is pushed aside in favor of other "more pressing" tasks.

Over the years, I've tried different ways to carve out a special time with the Lord. For a while, I read my Bible before going to bed. I found, however, that I was too tired to concentrate on what I was reading. More often than not, I flopped immediately into bed and never opened my Bible.

I also tried to set aside a few minutes during the day while the kids were at school. Although wide awake, I was distracted by the long list of chores and I easily found excuses to ignore this quiet time.

The best time I've found to be in the Word is when the day is brand-new. Setting my alarm so I awaken about an hour ahead of my family ensures a personal time with God so He can satisfy my spiritual hunger. The house is quiet— no voices to tune out, no phone calls to answer, and no chores to complete. It's the ideal time to visit with the Lord and start the day on the right foot.

It doesn't matter what time of day you choose to study God's Word and eat of this spiritual food. God has planned a rich feast for all of us and desires that we attend the banquet. Through the gift of faith in Jesus, we can pull up a chair and dine with the Lord here on earth and forever in heaven.

Jesus, thank You for removing the obstacles so I can be God's daughter. The forgiveness and life that are mine because of Your death and resurrection leap from the pages as I read God's Word. Fill me with a hunger to know more about Your actions on my behalf. As I continue to explore the Word, send Your Holy Spirit to keep me strong in faith and willing to share the Good News with others. Amen.

N.O.B.

Love Knots

~tie your love together with these ideas

Fuel Your Faith

1. **Church faith.** Placing us in a community of faith is one way the Lord strengthens our faith life. In this group we can hear and study God's Word, partake of the sacraments, and participate in worship and fellowship. Attend worship services regularly as a family. As appropriate, discuss the faith you confess, what God does for us in baptism and communion, the reality of sin, the grace of God, the promise of eternal life, the Trinity, etc. Gear your discussions to the age of your daughter, remembering that young children have difficulty understanding abstract concepts.

2. **Family faith.** Share with your daughter stories that have been passed from generation to generation about faithful men and women. Make her aware of how God helped her ancestors. Share stories from the present day as well— times God has helped you grow or has demonstrated His presence to you. If you haven't already done so, begin a family devotional time. You might use a devotion book and include singing, Scripture memorization, or re-enactments of Bible stories.

3. **Interceding faith.** Develop a family prayer board. Write individual prayer concerns on slips of paper and tack them to a bulletin board. List the names of people for whom you want to pray, including family members, church or school friends, missionaries, etc. When possible, include pictures. Include items for which to thank God. Ask your daughter to update this board with new requests and ways God has answered your prayers.

4. **Singing faith.** The church has a rich tradition of music. Learn songs of faith together. As you do so, discuss the meaning of the words. How does the writer's choice of Scripture passages or biblical concepts emphasize or highlight the truths of God's Word?

5. **Future faith.** Pray aloud for your daughter's future, beginning at her birth. When you pray, be sure she hears you and/or knows your concerns—for school, husband, job, church, friendships, children, etc. Thank God for the ways You see Him at work in her life.

6. **Basic faith.** It's never too early to begin reading from the Bible to your child. As a baby, introduce the stories of creation, Noah, Christmas, and Easter by using simple picture books. As your child grows in years and cognitive ability, challenge her with more in-depth accounts until she is capable of reading from the Bible with you.

7. **Biblical faith.** Talk with your daughter about one of your favorite Bible verses. Explain why it is important to you. Explain how God has opened your eyes to His ways as you have studied this verse. Work together to memorize Bible verses on a regular basis.

8. **Vocalize your faith.** Many people are nervous about praying out loud. To help your daughter avoid fear, encourage her to pray aloud often, including at the dinner table and at bedtime. Invite her to write out her prayer and read it if this is more comfortable for her. Pray aloud as a family during your devotion time, encouraging one another to express what is in your hearts.

9. **Continuously praying faith.** God invites us to pray without ceasing and give Him praise in all circumstances. One way to do this is to offer short prayers that come as naturally as breathing. For example, "Thank You, God, for this beautiful day!" or "Lord, keep us safe as we travel." Help your daughter see God throughout her daily life and celebrate His presence in every circumstance.

10. **Celebrating faith.** Make a "faith quilt" with your daughter or mother. Collect a favorite Scripture verse from each family member (include the men!). Either paint or embroider the verses on squares of fabric. Sew the squares into a quilt top. You can either complete the piece as a quilt or make it into a simple wall hanging. This could be an ideal gift for a special occasion, such as a marriage, anniversary, or birthday.

SPECIAL TIMES

Prayer

Lord of all,

Thank You for the special times You bring into our lives.

Thank You for the "dreaming times" when we wrap our arms around each other and survey the world and all You offer. Times when my daughter dreams of the future and I dream of the past. Times when together we use the gifts You have given us.

Thank You for the "surprising times"—big surprises and small, like when my daughter volunteers to do the dishes while I relax. And thank You for the privilege of spending time with my daughter enjoying an impromptu snack as we talk about things only girls can appreciate.

Thank You for the "challenging times"—even times of discouragement and fear. These are the times when You teach me that You have supplied all I need in the Person of Jesus, my Savior. Through His saving work, You have given me assurance to replace doubt, humility to replace pride, and forgiveness to replace anger.

Thank You for the "growing times." Times when I'm desperate and the right words come from her mouth. Times when I can point my daughter in Your direction. Times of stretching our wings to serve You and others even as we learn more about each other and You.

Thank You for the "faithful times"—when we confront surprises, challenges, opportunities for growth, and dreams with a faith in You that is rich, full, and overflowing. Remind us always that the faith we have is a gift from You—precious because of the cost. Keep us strong in the assurance of Your faithful presence in our lives. Amen.

Loosening the Ties (Just a Little)

And He took the children in His arms,
put His hands on them and blessed them.
Mark 10:16

I didn't want her to leave. I wanted to put her clothes back in the closet, her CDs back on the shelf, and her stuffed animals back on the bed where they'd been since she was little. Instead, I put a smile on my face and helped her load her car with several suitcases and boxes of essentials.

Katie was leaving for college. She wasn't the first to leave, but that's what made it hard. She was the last! What was I going to do without a child in the house? It would be too quiet without her music, too dull without her friends dropping by, and far too easy to make a telephone call.

For the first couple of weeks, I did not know what to do. I resisted the impulse to call her every hour, but I did send funny cards featuring various artists' interpretations of pigs, which Katie likes to collect. I spent days planning a special meal for her first day back home and nights worrying about what might happen to her. I knew she was having the time of her life, finally free from parental constraints. My mind settled on the frightening prospects of late hours, a poor diet, terrible study habits, and too many readily available cars. I told myself this was ridiculous, but I wasn't listening.

One day I dropped by the church to make some copies. As I walked past the sanctuary, I stepped inside the open doors. I liked the sanctuary when no one else was there. It was so different from the room's Sunday ambiance. There were no families worshiping in the pews, no one singing in the choir ... just quietness, and me, and God.

I recalled a time several years earlier when I had worked at the church as a part-time secretary. After everyone else had left for the morning, I had slipped inside the sanctuary and fallen on my knees at the altar. I asked God for the courage and trust to give my children to Him. I think that must be the hardest task for a mother—to leave her children in God's hands. But God answered my plea.

Now as I sat in the empty sanctuary and recalled the peace and the unwavering confidence that God would care for my kids that I had felt that day, I wondered when I had taken over again. I didn't remember a particular time that I decided that I had to worry about them, that I was the only one who could care for them and love them.

"Forgive me, Father," I whispered. "I give Katie back to You. I give them all back to You. As much as I love them, I know You love them more. You created them. Your Son gave His life to redeem them. Help me remember that You will take care of them, and help me to trust You."

A peace came back into my life as I released my grip on my children. When Katie came home for a visit, full of plans for the future and excitement about the new friends she had made, I wanted to pick up the reins again. I wasn't sure I wanted her to have friends I'd never met or make plans without consulting me. But I remembered Who was looking out for her, and I smiled as she shared her thoughts.

Thank You, God, for helping me to trust You, even when it seems difficult to do so. Thank You for providing for my every need, including my need for a Savior. In Jesus' name. Amen.

L.T.

Surprise!

*Now glory be to God who by His mighty
power at work within us is able to do far
more than we would ever dare to ask or
even dream of—infinitely beyond our
highest prayers, desires, thoughts, or
hopes. Ephesians 3:20 (TLB)*

Red, yellow, and blue helium-filled balloons bounced in
the breeze as I held them tightly while leaving the grocery
store. After putting the ice cream, soda, and chips in the
trunk of the car, I wrestled the balloons into the front seat.

A woman getting out of the car beside me smiled and
said, "I bet you're going to have a good time today!" Indeed
I was. It was Jennifer's 12th birthday, and I'd invited nine of
her friends for a surprise party that afternoon.

My original plans hadn't included the "surprise" part.
Jennifer wanted to have friends over to celebrate, but she
couldn't decide what kind of a party to have. At the ripe old
age of 12, she was well beyond the organized party at
America's number 1 hamburger place. My preteen didn't
want to hold a party at the roller rink or at the video
arcade. And with no swimming pool to entertain guests on a
hot afternoon, the idea of having a birthday bash at home
didn't appeal to her either. So what was a girl to do?

Nothing. Absolutely nothing. But I would have a surprise party and plan it all. Jennifer could just enjoy herself
and not worry about the details.

I felt quite mischievous. The week before the party, I

super-sleuthed around Jennifer's room to find the telephone numbers of her friends. When she was in the shower, I rushed to my bedroom to call each girl secretly. While she was in school, I combed the stores for cool prizes for the games and for the rest of the party necessities.

When the day of the party arrived, I baked, finished cleaning, and got the gift bags together. I hid the balloons in my shower stall, the games and gifts under my bed, and the brownies in the oven. It was nerve-wracking, yet exhilarating. I was really looking forward to the party.

Later that day, Jennifer left with Kimberly for what she thought was a sleepover. Within a half hour, the guests arrived and we decorated the house. Jennifer and Kimberly arrived back at my doorstep about an hour later.

"Shhh," I warned the room full of girls. They muffled their giggles as I opened the door.

Jennifer handed me an envelope. "Kimberly's mom forgot to give this to you," she said.

"Well, it's a good thing you came back because you forgot something," I said as I pointed to the living room floor.

Jennifer looked puzzled, but she stepped inside. At that moment the girls jumped out and yelled, "Surprise!"

My birthday girl froze. Her jaw dropped, and she stood there, wide-eyed and unable to speak. (A real miracle for a 12-year-old, you know.)

It was great! I'd pulled off the surprise of a lifetime. And I had managed to do it right! Afterward Jennifer told me that everything was perfect—from the guest list to the games. (No small feat when you're dealing with adolescents.)

My daughter is precious to me, and I want the best for

her. When she asked for a party with her friends, I gave her a super party with her closest friends. I didn't do it to outdo anyone; I did it because I love her.

God is the same way with us but on a much larger scale. As Ephesians 3:20 tells us, our heavenly Father wants to give us gifts so grand that we can't even begin to imagine them! But they don't always jump out and yell, "Surprise!" Sometimes His gifts are subtle like a beautiful sunset, a singing bird, or a visit from a dear friend. Sometimes the unfathomable importance of God's greatest gift to us—His Son—surprises us. This Jesus gave His life for our forgiveness, and through His resurrection, we have the gift of eternal life. What a gift!

You are one of God's gifts too. He created you for Himself and for others. Why not make today an Ephesians 3:20 day for your daughter or mother? Surprise her with the gift of your time and love.

Heavenly Father, help me see the gifts of Your hand today and celebrate Your love in all that I do. Amen.

N.O.B.

Moving Day

*The LORD'S curse is on the house of the
wicked, but He blesses the home of the
righteous. Proverbs 3:33*

I was glad when I had an opportunity to move to
Spindale, North Carolina, with my two daughters Robin
and Mary. It seemed like home from the beginning. Since
my Air Force family had constantly been on the move, I
never felt like I had a home. I wanted it to be different for
my children. I wanted them to have roots and friends and
neighbors they knew all their lives. It didn't take long for
this friendly town in the foothills of the Blue Ridge
Mountains to win my affection. I never wanted to move
again.

But that changed. When Earl and I married, we lived in
his house in Spindale for several years, but one of his dreams
always had been to move to the country. Within a few years,
we bought a small farm, sold our house in town, and moved
to the outskirts of the county. When our third child came
along, the farm house that came with the land became far
too small for our family of five. We began to make plans to
add a room or two.

One day, Earl came home from work with what he considered wonderful news. If we could find a way to move it,
we could have a building in town that was going to be torn
down. So began the most arduous moving day of my life. If I
thought it was tough moving from town to town or country

to country in my younger days, I obviously had never tried to move a building.

For weeks, Earl and I went over and jacked up the building, inch by inch. Then the driver we hired arrived and backed the truck under the building. We lowered the building onto the truck's bed. Once the building was loaded, the driver cruised down the highway and bounced across the ruts and tracks of the surrounding fields to deposit the building beside our house.

Eventually, the newly acquired building added two very large rooms to our house, becoming an integral part of the structure. And in the years since that move, several more rooms have been added, blending in as though they had always been there. Today our home sits pleasantly along the hillside, providing more than enough room for the whole family.

I realize today that "home" has nothing to do with the location or the size of a house. The small farm house welcomed us, spread its wings, and covered our growing family. I am thankful for a larger home and for nicer furnishings than we had in the beginning, but I am most grateful that God lives in our home—and that He's never going to move.

Thank You, Lord, for bringing us into Your family through Jesus, our Savior. May my "home" be wherever You are. Reside with us and in us. Thank You for being faithful and dependable. May we stand upon the solid Rock forever. Amen.

L.T.

Totally Terrific Me!

But my dove, my perfect one, is unique,
the only daughter of her mother, the
favorite of the one who bore her.
Song of Songs 6:9

Third grade was a very good year for Jennifer. Some special friends were in her class, and she adored her teacher, Cathy Anderson. I appreciated Mrs. Anderson as well, especially because she did all she could to help the children feel good about themselves.

Having positive self-esteem is important. I know that if Jennifer feels good about herself as a forgiven child of God, she'll be less likely to cave in to peer pressure and do something detrimental to herself or to another. At home, I try to bolster her self-esteem at every opportunity.

Because Mrs. Anderson wanted her students to learn more about each other and to feel good about who they were, she taught a unit called "Totally Terrific Me!" Every child got a turn to bring in pictures of themselves and their family. The photographs were displayed on the "Totally Terrific Me!" bulletin board, along with a letter written by the child's parent telling why this child was so terrific.

When it was Jennifer's turn, I wanted her letter to be something she could put in her scrapbook and cherish forever. This is what I wrote.

Dear Jennifer,

We were overjoyed the day you were born! We had waited six years since Matthew was born to be able to have another baby. You were a special gift from God, and we knew our life would be blessed by having you in our family.

You entered the world screaming! We were so happy to hear our child scream. Why? Because you were born four-and-a-half weeks premature. The special doctors warned us that you may not be breathing when you were born. They were prepared to do everything possible to save you. But they never had to do a thing. You were perfectly healthy and breathed a scream right away. You weighed 4 pounds, 15 ounces. You were tiny!

Jennifer, I think you are a terrific child for many, many reasons. The number one reason is because you are YOU—a very special creation God made in His image. We love you just because you are ours, but we think you do terrific things too.

You have wonderful musical abilities. You are a good singer, ballet dancer, and will someday be a fine musician because you have an "ear" for music. Daddy and I are always proud of you when we watch you perform at your ballet recital and when you sing in the children's choir at church.

You are kind to animals and take good care of our puppy, Suzy. You are also considerate of other people and seem to understand when someone is feeling sad. It means a lot to me when you put your arms around me and tell me, "I love you, Mommy." It always makes me feel better.

You seem to enjoy writing and I know that someday you will have a story published just like me. I know that a lot of my ideas have come from something you have said or done and we have been proud of the story when it's finished. Thanks, Jen!

I could tell all your classmates that you do a good job with your chores, you help Daddy outside, you help me clean the aquarium, and a bunch of other things. But they probably already know how helpful you are because I'm sure they see you help your friends and Mrs. Anderson. They are lucky children to know you.

Jennifer, I hope that you will remember each day of your life that you are totally terrific! No matter what you do or where you go, Daddy, Matthew, and I will always love you and will always think you're special—just because you're you!

Love,
Mommy

Has it been a while since you told your daughter or mother just how special she is? Perhaps today would be a good day to sit down and write her a letter and tell her how totally terrific she is—to you and to God!

O Creator, I'm so grateful to be the apple of Your eye. Help me to value the wonderful qualities You have given to others. Thank You for making me totally terrific through Jesus' death and resurrection. In my Savior's name. Amen.

N.O.B.

The Spirit of Thanksgiving

Let us come before Him with thanksgiving and extol Him with music and song.
Psalm 95:2

Thanksgiving is traditionally spent in our farmhouse with family members squeezed into every nook and cranny of the modest rooms. Our guest list usually includes Robin, Joe, and their three children; Mary, Gary, and their five kids; Katie and her boyfriend; Andy and his wife; David and his family; and Arthur and his wife, Debbie. And there's usually a friend or two thrown in for good measure.

We cook from early in the morning until it's time for lunch. Turkey, dressing, giblet gravy, ham, green beans, fruit salad, corn, cranberry sauce, hot buttered rolls, and iced tea are just a few of the items on the table.

A cool autumn breeze tosses golden leaves outside the window, but the house is warm and snug. "Happy Thanksgiving!" everyone greets everyone else as they come in the door. The younger adults are thankful to be off work for the day, and the older adults are thankful to have the whole family around. The teenagers are thankful that the football game will soon be on TV, and the children are thankful that their cousins are around to play with. The smells from the kitchen fill the house and entice child and adult alike to steal a bite or two as they pass the rapidly filling dining room table.

When it's time to eat, everyone fills their plate and

gathers in small groups all over the house to fellowship and eat. The young children sit around the coffee table, and the teenagers scatter throughout the living room, balancing their plates on their laps. The kitchen and dining room are filled with adults. The current baby occupies the old family high chair. We laugh and talk and enjoy the special meal together, but do we really think about the special time called Thanksgiving?

Once Katie reminded me to think about it. She was about 3 years old. The table was practically bowing under the load of food. Katie sat in the high chair, her plate of food untouched in front of her. She watched as brothers and sisters, cousins, aunts and uncles, and Mama and Daddy chatted and laughed their way through the food line. " 'appy Thanksgivin'!" she told everyone as they passed her chair.

Finally she called out, "Mama." I smiled at her as I slipped past to take hot rolls out of the oven.

"Mama!" she said a bit more insistently.

"What is it?" I called out over the bodies between us.

"Mama, can we have 'appy Thanksgivin' again tomor-row?" she asked. Suddenly the clatter and chatter stopped. Everyone turned to look at the small blonde, blue-eyed child.

"What did you say?" I asked.

"Can we have 'appy Thanksgivin' again tomorrow?" she repeated. "And the next day and the next and the next ..."

I began to explain that Thanksgiving came only once each year. "We can't have a meal like this every day. We'd all gain a hundred pounds and have great big tummies." I tickled her soft, warm stomach. Giggling, she squirmed away from my fingers. "And besides, everyone has to go back to work." By then the others had returned to their main occupation for the day: eating.

Seeing the concern on her young face, I knelt beside her. "But why not, Mama?" Katie asked. "It's so much fun!"

And she was right. It was fun. Not because it was a day off work or because there were wonderful football games and parades on television. Not even because of the food. But because everyone was there: brothers and sisters, cousins, aunts and uncles, and parents. And everyone was happy, which can sometimes be a rare event in the life of a large family.

I looked around and realized we needed to spread out the Thanksgiving spirit, somehow make it stretch from one November to the next. And I've consciously tried to do that. Sometimes I extend the spirit by inviting everyone for a meal. Sometimes it's simply pausing each morning to thank God for my personal blessings. Katie taught me that the spirit of Thanksgiving has nothing to do with full tables, football games, parades, or days off work. It has everything to do with appreciating the blessings God has given us, especially family, love, and the saving faith we have in Jesus.

Thank You, God, for the many blessings You shower on me. Thank You for my family and friends and the lessons You teach me through them. Help me thank You every day for Your greatest gift to me—my salvation. Amen.

L.T.

Were You Thinking What I Was Thinking?

*For who among men knows the thoughts
of a man except the man's spirit within
him? ... But we have the mind of Christ.
1 Corinthians 2:11, 16b*

Usually Jennifer sits next to me at church every week.
One Sunday, however, my husband, Mike, sat between us.

As we listened to our minister give the children's ser-
mon, his message about being wounded reminded me of a
devotion I'd written for this book ("When Is a Boo-Boo Not
a Boo-Boo?"). Although I couldn't nudge Jennifer or even
see her face, I was quite sure that she was thinking about
the devotion too.

After the service, our family ate lunch at a favorite
restaurant. While waiting for our food, I asked Jennifer what
I thought was a simple question: "Were you thinking what I
was thinking when Pastor Myric gave the children's ser-
mon?"

Jennifer smiled and replied, "Yeah, and I knew you were
thinking what I was thinking!"

I chuckled. "I just knew that you knew that I was thinking what you were thinking," I said.

At this point, Mike and Matthew wore puzzled expressions on their faces. Finally Mike asked, "Was there a conversation that just went on here?"

Jennifer and I laughed, knowing a very real dialogue

had indeed been going on. Our mother-daughter bond has become so strong that sometimes we can communicate and fully understand each other without a lot of words. We sense—we just know—what the other is thinking. It's a mother-daughter thing, a God-given bond that connects us.

This wonderful communication happens often. Many times I know what Jennifer is talking about before she even finishes her sentence. This ability baffles Mike and Matthew. Our conversations at the dinner table are a good example and might go something like this:

"I tripped and fell while we were playing basketball in P. E. today," Jennifer says and grins.

I smile. (I already know what she means.) "On purpose?" I ask.

"No, it just happened. But it was great," she says.

I raise my eyebrows. Jennifer giggles. I can see the wheels turning in Mike's head. He's wondering: *Why are they smiling? Didn't Jennifer say she tripped and fell down? I don't get it.*

"What?" Mike finally asks in desperation. Matthew just stares.

"Oh, Daddy," Jennifer scolds. She glances at me with a questioning look that asks, *Should I explain it to him—again?*

I nod. With that affirmation, she reminds her father that a boy helped her up when she fell last time, and he helped her this time too. (Now, why couldn't he have figured that out?)

There is a wonderful tie that binds women together. It comes from deep within us and is as natural as drawing a breath. Yes, there are special gifts God has given women such as intuition and a more relational nature. But, as Christians, we have an added bonus.

All Christians, male and female, have a tie that binds them together. It is Christ. The gift of faith, the washing of the waters of Baptism, the cleansing in the blood of Christ, unite us as brothers and sisters in Christ. We are the kingdom of God, and He has given us His Holy Spirit to draw us together. Because of the faith we share, we have the same goals, the same desires, the same hopes.

Is it any wonder, then, that the Creator who can tie together thousands upon thousands in the faith can also tie together the hearts of a mother and a daughter?

Dear God, thank You for Your Holy Spirit that connects me to You and to my daughter. In Jesus' name. Amen.

N.O.B.

A Time for Everything

Children's children are a crown to the aged, and parents are the pride of their children. Proverbs 17:6

It was hard to believe that my babies were going to have babies. My two older daughters were pregnant. I was going to be a grandma! Horror of horrors, I wasn't sure I liked the idea!

Everyone was supposed to like being a grandma. My own grandma had thought there was nothing more wonderful than her grandchildren. My older friends who already had grandchildren were thrilled. So what was wrong with me? It wasn't that I didn't want grandchildren. I just didn't want to be a *grandma.* "Why isn't there a way to have one without being the other?" I mumbled to myself when no one was listening. After all, my grandma had been old and I certainly wasn't old!

As the months passed, I poked fun at the way I felt. I was thrilled about the two young ones that would soon arrive, but somewhere inside, I was a little troubled. I didn't understand where my life had gone. Just yesterday, I was a new mother myself.

All that changed a few weeks later when I stood beside the hospital bed and gazed proudly at my brand-new grandson in Robin's arms. It changed again a few months later when I was privileged to go into the delivery room with Mary and see her son born. I'd always known babies were miracles, but I didn't know how miraculous they were until I saw my two daughters holding their sons.

I still wasn't satisfied with my new "title," however—not until the morning that I read the third chapter of Ecclesiastes for my devotions. I read: "There is a time for everything, and a season for every activity under heaven: a time to be born and a time to die, a time to plant and a time to uproot" (vv. 1–2). That made sense. I knew all about planting and uprooting from living on a farm. When the season was over, we pulled the beans up by their roots so new crops could be planted. This wasn't taking anything away from the colorful jars of beans that we put up in the pantry. It simply left room for new growth.

I continued reading: "a time to kill and a time to heal, a time to tear down and a time to build" (v. 3). When we moved to the farm, we tore down some buildings and replaced them with stronger structures that were better able to withstand storms. But we used the foundations of the old buildings for the new ones. Those babies were going to need a strong foundation on which to grow, one that only a grandparent could provide.

At last I was beginning to understand. As the Scriptures said, this was a time to laugh and dance, a time to embrace and speak of the wonderful blessings God had given in these two children, a time to love, a time for peace, and a time for growing in the knowledge of Jesus, our Savior.

A few days later, Mary came home from the hospital with Matthew and Robin brought Luke to meet his new cousin. As I observed the introduction, I slipped my arms around both girls and their sons. "I have only one request," I told them. "Do you think the boys could call me

Grandmother instead of *Grandma?*" I still wasn't quite ready to transform into the "Grandma" image, but I was more than willing to be the best "Grandmother" I could be.

> *God, teach me that the different stages of life are graced*
> *with their own individual strengths and treasures.*
> *Help me to make the most of each day, not looking*
> *backward or forward, but enjoying the blessings You*
> *give for that day. In Jesus' name. Amen.*

L.T.

"Thanks, Mom!"

How great is the love the Father has lav-
ished on us. 1 John 3:1

It had been one of those days. Everything that could go wrong did: my car got a flat (and it was my turn to drive the car pool), the washing machine broke, and our new puppy made a mess in the house.

By four o'clock that afternoon, I was ready to crawl into bed and possibly never come out from beneath the covers. Instead, I helped Jennifer with her homework, made dinner for my always hungry family, and prepared my notes for a meeting I had to conduct later that evening.

While I hacked a carrot into a million pieces for the salad, I thought about the hard parts of motherhood. Dashing from one task to another, driving children to and from activities, and doing the work of both maid and cook had left me feeling unappreciated, even unloved. After all, don't we believe that if our husbands and children love us, they will automatically gush with gratitude? Sure we do, at least some of the time. Normally, though, we realize that this mothering job is a thankless one. We do it because we love our family and know, deep down, that we are loved and appreciated, even if we don't hear it enough.

By the time I got home from my meeting, I was over-tired and had a massive headache. It was late, and Mike and the kids already had gone to bed. I was grateful for the silence as I put my purse and keys down on the kitchen table. On the table was a sheet of notebook paper with Jennifer's handwriting across it. I thought it was homework that my fourth-grader had left for me to look over. When I picked it up, I saw it was addressed to me. It read:

> Dear Mom,
>
> Thanks for all the things that you have done for me. I want you to know that I really love you! You are a number 1 parent and nobody could ever replace you.
>
> I didn't break anything or get in trouble. I just want you to know that I really love you! You are special and wonderful and the greatest mother on all the earth.
>
> Love,
> Jennifer
>
> P.S. I am glad that God made you!

Tears of thanksgiving made their way down my cheeks. I reread the letter, then walked to Jennifer's room. She was fast asleep. I sat on the edge of her bed, careful not to wake her. As I listened to the soft rhythm of her breathing, I brushed aside a long strand of brown hair from her face. I felt the tension in my neck and shoulders relax, my headache subside, and my breathing slow to a more normal pace.

Jennifer's note was the perfect ending to an otherwise awful day. Although I knew she loved me, it was nice to read it. Sitting in the dark, I thanked God for my daughter's love.

How long had it been since I told my family how much

I loved and appreciated them? I was humbled by the thought. After all my grumbling, I was just as guilty as the people I had criticized. When was the last time I thanked Mike for faithfully taking out the garbage? Or when had I thanked the kids for doing their chores? Or when had I given Jennifer a hug just because I loved her? And when was the last time I told God how much I appreciated the many ways He blessed us? When I thought about it, I realized it had been awhile.

I softly kissed Jennifer goodnight and left her room. *I'm so grateful for my daughter, Lord,* I silently prayed while walking back to the kitchen.

My earlier revelation replayed in my mind. I looked at the clock. Now was a good time. Knowing that my mother usually stayed up late, I dialed her number.

"Hi, Mom," I said when she answered. "It's me. I just wanted to call and tell you how much I love you …"

Father, through Your Spirit, help me to show love and gratitude to all who pass my way but especially to those I see every day. I want to share this love in response to the tremendous love You showed to me when You sent Jesus to earth to be my Redeemer. In His name I pray. Amen.

N.O.B.

He Hurts When We Hurt

Jesus wept. John 11:35

It is a regrettable fact that at least one person sitting in almost every high school freshman orientation class will die before that class graduates. It has been true for my children. One of Mary's friends died of cancer. Three of Andy's football buddies died on the afternoon of the first day of school in a car accident. Katie's friends, identical twin girls, died early one morning on their way to school when they pulled out in front of a truck.

Robin was the first of my children to experience this kind of loss. One of her friends, a beautiful young woman with a bright future, was killed when her car overturned and rolled on her. I was at a loss as to how I could help Robin or her friends through the grieving process.

"Why, Mama?" Robin asked. "Why would something like this happen?"

"I don't know," I told her, angry myself at the senseless death. I felt badly for the woman's parents and her brother and for my own daughter, who had lost a friend.

Robin was 16 at the time, but she had seen death before. She had seen elderly neighbors and her great-grandmother and grandfather pass away, but they had lived a full life. "She was only 16," Robin said quietly as she turned to leave the room. "She had her whole life before her."

As the funeral approached, I wanted to help Robin, but how could I when I had no answers myself. I tried not to let her see the tears in my eyes because I didn't want to upset her further. But as she was getting ready to go to the church, Robin turned to me and said, "Mama, Betsy was a Christian, and I know she's with God now. But does that mean we're not supposed to be sad?"

"No, honey, I don't think so," I answered. "In fact, remember what you learned about Lazarus in Bible school. Lazarus and his sisters, Martha and Mary, were good friends of Jesus. Doesn't the Bible say that Jesus cried when Lazarus died?"

"Yes," she said, laughing a little at the memory of sitting with her friends around a small table in the Sunday school room with Kool-Aid on one side and cookies on the other. "I even remember the verse. It says 'Jesus wept.' That's the shortest verse in the Bible, and the one we all wanted to use for our memory verse."

"You're right," I said, also smiling at the memory. "It is the shortest verse, but it may be the most profound. Do you think Jesus was crying because His friend died?"

"Probably not. He knew that He could bring Lazarus back to life," Robin said. She thought for a moment, then turned to me with a new light in her eyes. "I think He was crying because He felt badly for Mary and Martha."

"I think you're right," I told her. "Even though Betsy is in heaven with Jesus right now, He understands our loss and pain."

"Mama, do you think Jesus is crying now?" she asked, tears beginning to fill her eyes.

"I think maybe He is," I told her as I put my arms around her. We both sat on her bed, held each other, and cried until the tears were gone.

I was proud of the way Robin and her friends reached out to Betsy's parents, not only during the funeral but later on special days and at graduation. I was proud of my other children when similar events happened in their circle of friends.

The death of a friend is never easy whether we're young or old, but it does help to know Jesus understands and hurts with us.

Father, even though I'm Your child, sometimes I don't understand things like the death of a loved one. In moments like these, take me in Your arms, hold me, and let me cry out my fears and heartaches. Remind me again of the sure hope of the resurrection that is mine for Jesus' sake. Thank You for understanding all my hurts and for being my great Healer. In my Savior's name. Amen.

L.T.

Legacy of Love

You have given me the heritage of those
who fear Your name. Psalm 61:5

I love antiques! Although some people think they're
junk, to me they're precious and tell a story of a bygone
time. The pieces I love the most are those that have been
handed down from generation to generation within my family.

Because my maternal grandparents knew of my great
love and appreciation for antiques, they gave me many heirlooms. In fact, Grammy and Pop Pop gave me anything that
was "old" and had some family value to it.

When Jennifer was in kindergarten, she showed an
interest in the heirlooms and asked me to tell her about
some of my treasures.

"What's this bucket for?" she asked as she pointed to a
white enamel pail.

"When your great-grandfather was a little boy, he lived
in New York City. Back then, people got their milk from the
milkman. He had big containers of milk on his horse-drawn
wagon. Pop Pop would give this pail to the milkman to fill.
Then he'd take it home to his mother."

"Neat," said Jennifer. "And his mother was Nana,
right?"

"That's right. And this was Nana's rocking chair," I said,
running my hand along the top of the rocker. "My mother
remembers Nana rocking her in this chair. It's very old."

Jennifer listened as I shared the stories behind the treasures. *Someday these reminders of past generations will be hers*, I thought. I knew Jennifer would appreciate each one and that she would tell her children about our family's heritage. But as I scanned the room, I wondered what I could pass on to my daughter.

After thinking about this for several weeks, I had a wonderful idea. I decided to have a portrait done of Jennifer and me. I called our favorite photographer and set up an appointment.

Because I wanted the portrait to have a timeless appeal, I decided we couldn't wear clothing that would identify the year or decade. I found just the right dress. It was an heirloom passed down to my minister's wife, and it fit me perfectly. The high neckline was topped off with fine lace. Mother-of-pearl buttons ran from top to bottom down the front of the dress, and delicate lace adorned the thin white fabric.

Jennifer wore a simple white slip with a satin ribbon in her long brown hair. She went barefoot. Barely 5 years old, she looked like a cherub.

I sat in my great-grandmother's rocking chair for the portrait, my wedding gown draped across my lap. Jennifer sat at my feet. The photographer caught me reaching to touch Jennifer's shoulder as she admired the gown that she might someday wear. On the floor next to Jennifer lay the gown I wore when I was christened. It is the same gown Jennifer wore at her christening.

Other treasures surrounded us: Grandma's old Bible, handmade doilies, two vintage photographs, and a lace handkerchief. All of these heirlooms, captured on canvas, remind me of my family and its rich heritage.

This portrait hangs in our living room with all the other heirlooms. Someday Jennifer will have this portrait to remind her of her mother's family. But in the seven years since the picture was taken, I've discovered that I have a far more precious legacy to pass on—my faith.

I hope my daughter will remember my love for God. She'll have my Bible, worn from years of use. She'll be able to thumb through its pages and read the underlined verses that meant so much to me, especially those that point to Jesus, our Good Shepherd, who gave His life for us. I know Jennifer will cherish her memories of our family worshiping together, praying around the kitchen table, and trusting the Lord during hard times. These memories will be a legacy that she can live out and pass on to her own children. And that will be worth more than any family heirloom she inherits. And as much as I love the portrait of my daughter and me, I can think of no better legacy to leave.

Dear Lord, thank You for our ancestors whom You called to be Your followers. Thank You for bringing us into Your family. Help us share the Good News of Your gift of faith with others. Amen.

N.O.B.

The Christmas Angel

They are like the angels. They are God's children. Luke 20:36

As coordinator of the children's Christmas program at church, I wanted to have record-breaking attendance. On the morning of the program, I noticed a new child and her mother worshiping with us. As we were going out the door, I invited them to join us for the program that night. The thin, dark-haired little girl, half-hidden behind her mother, stared at 12-year-old Robin and 9-year-old Mary with wide eyes.

The mother told us they would like to come, but she couldn't leave her ill husband that night. Before I could think of what to say, Mary and Robin already were telling the young girl that we would be picking up other children in the church bus. "We can pick her up too, can't we, Mama?" they chorused.

"Why ... why, yes," I mumbled half-heartedly, "Of course we can."

As I scribbled directions to the woman's house, I was thinking more about the things I had to do that afternoon than about the young girl. Props needed to be transported to the church. Costumes had to be prepared. Sandwiches needed to be made for the pre-program snack. Curtains had to be put up for the stage. And all this didn't take into account the other youngsters who had to be picked up from all over our neighborhood. And now I'd have to go clear across town to pick up this child.

Later that afternoon, Mary and Robin made space for the young girl on the seat between them as she climbed into the van. "How old are you?" Robin asked.

"Nine," she answered in barely more than a whisper.

When we arrived at the church, she followed the others inside and took a seat in the corner, quietly watching all that was going on.

"Mama," Mary said, pulling me over to the side. "Can't she be one of the angels?"

"She doesn't have a costume," I hedged.

"We could find something in the costume box for her to wear," Robin said.

"She won't know the songs," I said, my mind flying to find an excuse. *If I had time to practice the part with her, it would be different,* I argued to myself. We had worked so hard to make everything perfect, and she might not be able to sing.

Before I could refuse, though, Robin and Mary had pulled the girl into the next room. When they returned, she was draped in an old sheet with holes for her head and arms. They had pinned back her hair and strategically placed silver tinsel in her dark curls. She looked beautiful. My daughters lit up when they looked at her.

During the program, I listened in amazement as the young girl's voice blended beautifully with the chorus, even reaching out beyond them with a clearness and sweetness. Robin and Mary glanced at each other, smiled, and lifted their voices to join hers.

As I really listened for the first time that season to the angel's glorious message to the shepherds, God ushered the Christ Child into my heart. "Do not be afraid. I bring you good news of great joy that will be for all the people ... a Savior has been born to you" (Luke 2:10–11). As the children's voices spread throughout the auditorium, I knew that God had sent a beautiful Christmas angel to teach me about true joy.

Savior, thank You for allowing others to teach me.
Thank You for allowing me to reach others with Your
Good News. Remind me that it is more blessed to give
than to receive. Allow the message of the Christmas sea-
son to permeate my heart and remain with me through-
out the year. Amen.

L.T.

More Than Beautiful

I praise You because I am fearfully and
wonderfully made. Psalm 139:14

Call me biased, but I think my daughter has a lovely voice. When she was asked to sing a duet at church, I wanted her to not only sound beautiful but to look beautiful. So we discussed what she would wear.

"I want to wear the dress Nana gave me," she said.

"And your white socks with the lace would look good," I added.

"Mom!" she said in disgust. "I'm a big girl now. You need to buy me stockings."

Stockings? I thought. My little girl was growing up, and she wanted to feel pretty. I understood perfectly. I bought her stockings. I also ironed her dress, curled her hair, and let her wear a pair of my favorite earrings.

When Sunday arrived and her daddy saw her all dressed up, he said, "You look beautiful, honey."

Jennifer twirled in a circle and raised one hand above her head. "I'm more than beautiful!" she proclaimed. And she was right.

God made each of His children special and wants them to feel that way. But we ruined this specialness when we sinned. God, however, sent Jesus to restore this perfection through His perfect life, death, and resurrection. Because of Him, we are perfect in God's sight and can celebrate this every day.

*Heavenly Father, may my words and actions reflect the
new life that is mine through the gift of faith in Jesus.
Help me to build up others and stress the positive in
my interactions with family and friends. Amen.*

N.O.B.

Stormy Nights

He got up and rebuked the wind and the
raging waters; the storm subsided, and
all was calm. Luke 8:24b

It was Katie's graduation from R-S Central High
School, and the whole family would watch as she marched
across the stage in the football stadium. For Andy's graduation the previous year, it had rained, and the festivities had
to be moved inside the auditorium. That meant tickets had
to be rationed out for the much smaller seating space, and
only five family members had been able to attend.

We were relieved we wouldn't have to make choices
like that again. After all, we assured ourselves, even though
there had been light showers throughout the day and we
had received our five tickets just in case, it was surely not
going to rain again. That had never happened in the history
of graduations at Central.

Katie went early to gather with her class in the auditorium. The rest of us piled into the stadium to get a seat near
the front. Katie's boyfriend chatted with Andy and Christy
about the downpour last year. Mary and her family and
Robin and Jenny were joking about who would get the tickets if it rained. Earl was talking to the man behind him. I
was minding the umbrellas, anxiously glancing at the darkening skies.

The junior marshals passed out programs, and the stadium filled rapidly as the storm clouds approached. The wind

picked up, and the marshals scurried to recapture programs and the long ribbon that marked the path for the graduates. I passed out the umbrellas as it began to rain lightly. "Keep going, keep going," we urged the clouds. By this time, the marshals were wiping off the seats for the graduates. The principal had made several trips toward the microphone to move us inside, each time changing his mind.

Finally the band struck up the long-awaited march. We watched the faculty, dressed in navy blue robes, lead the seniors from the auditorium and onto the field. That's when the skies opened up and the storm struck. It seemed as if someone was standing over our heads pouring buckets of water directly onto us. Thankfully the seniors had barely left the auditorium. They assumed something was wrong when they saw their teachers, robes hiked up to their knees, running full speed into the building. While the teachers and graduates barely got their hair damp, the rest of us stood out in the deluge deciding who was going to get the five tickets.

Katie's night wasn't ruined, though. With rain dripping from our eyelashes and clothes clinging to our bodies, the choices were made about who went home and who stayed. Katie's boyfriend gallantly gave his ticket to Christy, then slipped in through another door and stood against a side wall to watch the ceremony.

It was a night to remember, and Katie was blissfully unaware of the confusion. As I sat in the auditorium seat, water still dripping from my clothes and hair plastered to my head, I watched her walk proudly across the stage. I forgot about the storm and reveled in the fact that our youngest daughter was graduating with honors. It was a wonderful night.

I wonder how many times we think, "Surely this won't happen," or "Certainly that won't occur." We think we can't bear another stormy night or turbulent day. Yet when the storms of life burst upon us, we can rest in the arms of the One whom even the wind and waters obey. God can calm more than just the storms of Galilee. He alone has the power to calm all the storms in our lives.

Lord, during the stormy days remind me that You are the Prince of Peace. I am thankful that Your peace does not depend on how I feel, but on what You have done on the cross to save me from myself, the devil, and this destructive world. Amen.

L.T.

A Tear for Joey

*Trust in the LORD with all your heart
and lean not on your own understanding. Proverbs 3:5*

"Mommy, I found out that Joey is moving away sometime after spring break," Jennifer told me one day before her
school vacation. Reading her solemn expression, I knew this
concerned her greatly. Joey was Jennifer's first childhood
sweetheart.

"I'm sorry, honey." I pulled her to me and hugged her
close. "I know how it feels when a special friend moves
away. It hurts at first, but then it gets better. You can always
write to him, you know."

"It won't be the same," she said with a sigh.

During moments like these, I feel inadequate as a parent. I wonder what I should say, knowing that my daughter
trusts me for the right answer. These are the times when I
wish God would just fix the problem. Not only would everything be perfect, but I would be off the hook as well.

The first day back to school after the break, Jennifer
came home in tears. Her lower lip quivering, she said, "Joey
moved during spring break, and I didn't get to say good-
bye." She sobbed in my arms, devastated that she hadn't
been able to see him one last time.

It was hard for me to handle too. I hated seeing my little girl upset. I found myself asking God, "Why couldn't You
have just let her say good-bye? Why did You let her get

hurt?" I begged God to show me a way to ease her pain.

For the rest of the week, Jennifer was quiet. Although I knew that in time she would feel better, I didn't know how to help her through her grief. No Scripture verse leaped off the pages of my Bible as an answer. No voice in the night told me what to do. As I looked to my heavenly Father, I heard no words of wisdom.

When Friday night arrived, I slipped into bed and longed to drift off to sleep where I could no longer see my daughter's sorrowful face or focus on my unanswered prayer.

As I lay quietly in bed, my mind replayed Jennifer's simple bedtime prayer. In her childlike faith, Jennifer trusted God to watch over her as she slept each night.

I knew I could trust God too. I decided to take Jennifer out to her favorite restaurant for breakfast in the morning. It would be a special treat for her, and I hoped that this time together would aid in her healing.

The next morning Jennifer was delighted to learn that we were going out to eat. As I enjoyed a leisurely breakfast, I began to relax. Jennifer's first heartbreak had to come at some point, and everything would work out in time.

As we were leaving the restaurant, Jennifer suddenly froze. Yanking at my arm, she said, "Mom, look! I can't believe it. It's Joey." I swung around and saw Joey and his family sitting in a nearby booth.

Walking up to their table, Jennifer said, "Joey, I—I thought you moved."

Joey's face lit up when he saw Jennifer. "I've been home this week packing. We're leaving today—right after breakfast," he said.

Jennifer gave Joey her address, and he promised to

write. Smiling at each other, both children seemed glad to have this opportunity to say good-bye.

I put my arm around Jennifer as we walked to our car. Looking down at her, I could see her eyes welling up with tears. Once inside the car, Jennifer wept. This time her tears were bittersweet. Although Joey was moving, she had been able to see him one last time.

As I held her, I thanked God for showing me another example of how He cares for a little girl's heart. And for her mother's as well.

Lord, remind us that You care for us in ways we don't even know about. When doubts creep in, point us again to Your promise of a Savior fulfilled in Jesus Christ. Amen.

N.O.B.

Love Knots

~tie your love together with these ideas

Celebrate Special Times

1. **Times to cherish family.** Plan a heritage portrait of you and your daughter or of you and your mother (or of all three generations!). Gather family heirlooms such as old clothes, furniture, or an old family Bible to use in the portrait. This makes a wonderful keepsake for future generations. Discuss the faith of your ancestors as you plan for this photo.

2. **Times to laugh.** Everyone needs a break from the humdrum of daily living, and it's true that "laughter is the best medicine." Have a "Joke Day" to share jokes, comics, or a funny movie with your daughter, granddaughter, or mother. Thank God together for times such as these.

3. **Times to remember.** Page through old photo albums, especially when you need a cuddly moment or a time to snuggle and share. Reflect on the ways God has been active in your life and the life of your daughter and mother. You might consider framing baptismal pictures of each generation as a special remembrance for the women in your family.

4. **Times to share abilities or talents.** Knit, crochet, or cook together. Ask Grandma to show you how to prepare a special family recipe or how to embroider or do counted cross stitch. As you work together, emphasize the wonderful gifts God has given each of you. Celebrate the blessing of time to be together.

5. **Times to reach out.** It's important for you to know your daughter's friends and for them to know you. Invite three of her favorite friends over to decorate cookies or cupcakes, then enjoy the fruits of your labor. You'll learn more about each other and what's going on in your different worlds. Beforehand, plan with your daughter at least one way to witness your faith to these friends.

6. **Times to explore.** Take up bird or butterfly watching together. Visit an aviary or a butterfly garden. Learn how to identify butterflies or birds and their calls. Discuss the many ways God has made each creature—including each person—unique.

7. **Times to say you care.** Develop a secret way of communicating with each other, such as using a "thumbs up" signal, winking, or by signing "I love you." These little affirmations help express your love, no matter where you are. List the many ways God tells you He cares and post the list on your refrigerator or family bulletin board.

8. **Times to play.** Play dolls with your young daughter. Use it as an opportunity to discuss mother/child love and to promote your little one's imagination. Gather clothes, costumes, jewelry, shoes, hats, and purses that your daughter or granddaughter can use to play "dress up." Encourage her to role-play situations in which she might witness her faith. Remind her that the Holy Spirit will be with her to guide her words and actions.

9. **Times to learn.** Visit the library or bookstore together. As you browse, share those books that grab your attention. If your daughter is young, plan time to read to her. If she is older, you each can read a book and discuss it later. Don't forget to visit your church library and local Christian bookstore. You could invest time in a Bible study or daily devotion time with your daughter and/or mother. This special time of learning about God would be an opportunity for the Holy Spirit to strengthen your spiritual bonds as well.

10. **Times to anticipate.** Countdown to a special day, such as a family birthday or a national holiday with a linked paper chain or a calendar you make together. You also can buy silly or inexpensive presents each day for the final week before the big day. This is especially appropriate for the season of Advent, which is a time of preparation for the celebration of the Savior's birth.

✿ *Wrap all these times with the ribbon of worship of our God, remembering who we are because of "Him who loved us and gave Himself up for us" (Ephesians 5:12).*

THE AUTHORS

Nancy Otto Boffo is a writer and contributing editor of Devo'Zine. *She has written articles for* Guideposts, Moody, *and* HomeLife, *and others.*

Linda Tomblin is a best-selling author and contributing editor of Guideposts. *She has written for* Reader's Digest, Today's Christian Parent, Today's Man, *and more.*